I0201805

ABUNDANCE

Faith & Wisdom
MOVING YOUR MOUNTAIN

by
stephanie
d. moore

"THE RIGHTEOUS MAN WILL FLOURISH LIKE THE PALM TREE,
HE WILL GROW LIKE A CEDAR IN LEBANON."
PSALM 92:12

WE MUST TRUST GOD, EMBRACE WISDOM & TAKE ACTION!

Copyright © 2017 by Stephanie D. Moore

Design: Moore Marketing and Communications, LLC
All rights reserved.

In accordance with the U.S. Copyright Act of 1976, scanning, uploading, or electronic sharing of any part of this book, audio, written, or e-published is strictly prohibited and unlawful. No part of this book may be reproduced in any form by any means, including photocopying, electronic, mechanical, recording, or by any information storage and retrieval systems without permission in writing by the copyright owner.

Published by
Moore Marketing and Communications
Oklahoma City, Oklahoma
www.StephanieDMoore.com

Bulk copies or group sales of this book are available by contacting moore@stephaniedmoore.com or by calling (405) 306-9833.

FIRST EDITION PRINTED NOVEMBER 2017
Printed in USA

Moore, Stephanie D.
Abundance: Faith & Wisdom - Moving Your Mountain. 31-Day Devotional
First Edition.

Library of Congress Control Number: 2017908212
1. Jesus 2. Abundance 3. Devotional 4. Spirituality 5. Religion 6. Christianity 7. God

Issued also as an ebook.

ISBN: 978-0-9962040-4-0

Abundance
31-Day Devotional

P_{AGE}

Faith & Wisdom: Moving Your Mountain   **5**

The Gift	11
Prophecy	19
Provision	23
Purpose	27
Protection	31
Faith	37
Love	45
Expectancy	51
Open Doors	57
Giving	65
Tithing	73
Investing	79
Saving	83
Anointing	89
Blessing	95
Praise	99
Gratitude	105
Jesus	111
Impossible	117
Elegant	121
Begin	125
Forget	131
Continue	137
Speak	143
A Table in the Presence of Your Enemies	147
Next	151
Abundance	155
Grace	161
Sacrifice	165
Joy	169
Eternal	175

Abundance   **179**

DEDICATED TO
MY GRANDMOTHER, BERTHA M. BRADLEY

"REJOICE EVERMORE.
PRAY WITHOUT CEASING.
IN EVERY THING GIVE THANKS:
FOR THIS IS THE WILL OF GOD IN CHRIST JESUS
CONCERNING YOU."

I THESSALONIANS 5:16-18

THERE IS NO BETTER TEACHER THAN JESUS CHRIST.
NO BETTER WORD THAT WHAT WE FIND IN THE BIBLE.
NO BETTER EXPERIENCE THAN THE LIFE
THAT WE LIVE EACH DAY.

WE OBTAIN AN ABUNDANCE OF HAPPINESS, STRENGTH AND
LOVE WHEN BEGIN TO BELIEVE THAT GOD <u>DESIRES</u> TO GIVE US
AN ABUNDANT LIFE.

WE <u>PROVE</u> THAT WE BELIEVE GOD AND HIS PROMISES BY
TAKING WISE ACTION.

ABUNDANCE

Faith & Wisdom

MOVING YOUR MOUNTAIN

by stephanie d. moore

AND ELIJAH SAID UNTO AHAB,
GET THEE UP, EAT AND DRINK;
FOR THERE IS A SOUND OF ABUNDANCE OF RAIN.

SO AHAB WENT UP TO EAT AND TO DRINK.
AND ELIJAH WENT UP TO THE TOP OF CARMEL;
AND HE CAST HIMSELF DOWN UPON THE EARTH,
AND PUT HIS FACE BETWEEN HIS KNEES,

AND SAID TO HIS SERVANT, GO UP NOW, LOOK TOWARD THE
SEA. AND HE WENT UP, AND LOOKED, AND SAID, THERE IS
NOTHING. AND HE SAID, GO AGAIN SEVEN TIMES.

AND IT CAME TO PASS AT THE SEVENTH TIME,
THAT HE SAID, **BEHOLD, THERE ARISETH A LITTLE CLOUD OUT
OF THE SEA, LIKE A MAN'S HAND.** AND HE SAID, GO UP, SAY
UNTO AHAB, **PREPARE THY CHARIOT, AND GET THEE DOWN
THAT THE RAIN STOP THEE NOT.**

AND IT CAME TO PASS IN THE MEANWHILE, THAT THE HEAVEN
WAS BLACK WITH CLOUDS AND WIND, AND THERE WAS A
GREAT RAIN. AND AHAB RODE, AND WENT TO JEZREEL.

AND THE HAND OF THE LORD WAS ON ELIJAH;
AND HE GIRDED UP HIS LOINS,
AND RAN BEFORE AHAB TO THE ENTRANCE OF JEZREEL.
I KINGS 18:41 - 46

**ABUNDANCE REQUIRES FAITH...
AND THE WISDOM TO TAKE ACTION.**

Faith & Wisdom
MOVING YOUR MOUNTAIN

"WHEN JESUS SAW HIM AND KNEW
HE HAD BEEN ILL FOR A LONG TIME,

HE ASKED HIM, **"WOULD YOU LIKE TO GET WELL?"**

"I CAN'T, SIR," THE SICK MAN SAID,
"FOR I HAVE NO ONE TO PUT ME INTO THE POOL WHEN THE
WATER BUBBLES UP. SOMEONE ELSE ALWAYS GETS THERE
AHEAD OF ME."

JESUS TOLD HIM,
"STAND UP, PICK UP YOUR MAT, AND WALK!"

INSTANTLY, THE MAN WAS HEALED!
HE ROLLED UP HIS SLEEPING MAT AND BEGAN WALKING!"
JOHN 5:6-9A

WE HAVE EVERYTHING WE NEED.

As long as we have Jesus Christ living on the inside of us, we have everything we need. God desires that we live an abundant life. Trusting him is the execution of faith.

It is our responsibility to chase every facet and detail required to make it happen and do the work. This is wisdom.

For many years, I knew I was supposed to be an author. God gave me the gift of storytelling. This is how and why I began my career in graphic design. I wanted to make the stories I wrote into animated movies. But, as I began to learn my craft, the business world offered me opportunities to grow and learn. I was intrigued and excited... like a little kid exploring every flavor available in a candy store. So, becoming an author would have to wait. **But, my dream never died.**

Instead, it grew and grew within me. One day, I couldn't take it anymore. I had to pick up my bed and walk. **It wasn't easy.** I faced enormous and seemingy insurmountable challenges every day.

In faith, I take all my needs and desires to God in prayer. Once delivered safely into his hands, I can release them and trust Him. That isn't easy either!

In wisdom, I research scripture for foundation and connect that to the required natural resources and relationships necessary to make what I hope for become reality. This requires an attitude of resilience and an ability to stay the course.

Finally, after I have done **everything** I can do, I lean, believe, confess and KNOW in my heart that Jesus will make it happen. This positive outlook encourages me to continue in faith during the days while I wait. I continue to believe and confess, **"I know God WILL move this mountain!"**

The Gift

"WHEN JESUS THEN LIFTED UP HIS EYES, AND SAW A GREAT
COMPANY COME UNTO HIM, HE SAITH UNTO PHILIP, WHENCE
SHALL WE BUY BREAD, THAT THESE MAY EAT? AND THIS
HE SAID TO PROVE HIM: FOR HE HIMSELF KNEW
WHAT HE WOULD DO."
JOHN 6:5-6

In Context

Jesus was teaching in Tiberias. About 5,000
people came to hear him speak. Jesus asked his
disciple Phillip, "Where can we buy bread to feed
the people?" He asked him this to test his faith.
But Phillip replied that they didn't have enough
money to feed the people. Andrew, another
disciple, knew there was a young man with a
small basket of bread and fish... while it was not
enough to feed 5,000 people, he told Jesus
about it.

Jesus instructed them to make the men sit.
He then gave thanks over the bread and fish
and had the disciples distribute it. There were
12 baskets left over and Jesus instructed they
gather that up.

Then the disciples waited until evening to cross over the sea. They got into a boat and crossed over and were 20 to 30 furlongs out when Jesus began walking on the water toward them. When they saw Jesus they became afraid. But he assured them it was ok. As soon as he got in the boat, they were at the destination.

Now the people at the destination were **surprised** to see Jesus with them because they knew the disciples left the other side alone and they thought Jesus stayed in Tiberias. So a person approached Jesus and said "Lord, I didn't see you come over on the side with your disciples how did you get here?"

Jesus left because he knew they wanted to make him king after the last miracle. He responded, **"You are striving for my presence because of the miracles, but rather than desire the bread that won't last, get the meat that won't perish, my Father in heaven has ordained me to provide."** Then they asked, "What shall we do that we may do the work of God?" Jesus responded, "The work of God is to believe in the one he has sent."

They referred to the raining of manna from Heaven to which Jesus responded that again their vision was skewed. The point of manna raining was to give homage to the God that provided it. In the same way, he continued, God was doing that through his life. He is the bread that God has provided to save lives. "If you walk with me, you don't get hungry or thirsty. I tell you this because even though you've seen me perform miracles you still don't believe. But, every person God has given to me will eventually **RUN** to me. And once I have them, I won't let go. (This made me laugh out loud in joy). I came do God's will, not my own."

His statements made the Jews angry. He then said that if a person trusts him and obeys him they enter into real life.

Then they openly began to doubt Jesus, touting his heritage questioning if anyone believed him. But Jesus put an end to their arguing assuring them, "I am the bread of life." He promised that if anyone believed in him they would learn from him as it is given to him directly from God. Then he told them that anyone who eats his flesh is consuming the bread of life. And anyone that drinks his blood is doing the same. The Jews were taken aback and offended. Jesus explained that by eating his flesh and drinking his blood we become one. They are in the Father and the Father is in them. His disciples were shocked as well. **But Jesus assured that man can do nothing in the flesh or simply by will power, that it is the Spirit that gives life.**

He lost several disciples that day. Then Jesus asked the twelve disciples, "Do you want to leave?" Then Peter responded, "Where would we go? You have the words of eternal life and we are committed. We know the Holy One is within you." Then Jesus said, "I handpicked you all, but one of you is a devil." Judas Iscariot was even then planning his betrayal.

Where would we go?

Jesus is my best friend.

He knows me better than I know myself. For a long time, I was lost and confused and making poor choices. It was just like it says in John 6, I ran to him. It was my only option. The obvious choice... and the best thing that ever happened to me.

Since then, Jesus has been calling me to walk on water - to demonstrate my faith before others in a crazy way. But just like the two fish and five loaves of bread, he has multiplied every area of my life.

He took my mediocre, no way to live life and he thanked God for it, then broke it... giving me to many and leaving nothing behind. I went from being a struggling coke addict to becoming a successful business owner. I have written more than seven books, launched an international girls program, a national male program and have a thriving marketing firm. I give and give and give until there is nothing left to brag about except the work of God through me.

I can't complain. My children are blessed. As I write, my 22-year old daughter is giving birth to my first grand baby, Levi! God is amazing and my walk with him is nothing short of adventurous, fulfilling and abundant... all because I chose to believe.

"GOD HAS GIVEN EACH OF YOU A GIFT FROM HIS GREAT VARIETY OF SPIRITUAL GIFTS. USE THEM WELL TO SERVE ONE ANOTHER."
I PETER 4:10

In Context
Christ was perfect and he suffered. We must suffer as well. Rather than live as before chasing mindless desires and worshiping false idols, we are called to change. Your friends may not agree and may even ridicule you but that is ok. Keep going. Before this world ends, and it will soon, learn to devote time and energy to disciplined intentional prayer.

Live life exhorting our spiritual gifts using those gifts to bless others. Live with God in the Spirit and let him flow through you. In this way, your life will bring God glory. **You can't be surprised at the trials you go through.** These trials are evidence that you are walking with Christ. Have joy and peace knowing that his glory will be revealed through you. However, don't allow your suffering come from causing trouble: murder, meddling, stealing or making trouble. There is no shame in suffering for Christ, instead praise God for he chastises those he loves first. If we are chastised for our sins, how much greatly will those without Christ suffer for their sin? If your suffering is pleasing to God, have faith and continue to trust him because God IS faithful.

Final Notes

Disciples of the Lord do what he instructs, even (or in most cases, especially) if it doesn't make sense. Our only job is to believe Jesus!

From trusting God to multiply meager scraps into a bountiful feast to leaving Christ alone while traveling on the boat and seeing him walk on the water... we are called to believe and trust God.

The crazy part of John 6 is that the people were ready to make Jesus their king but the minute he shared he was ordained by God to be more than king they rejected him. **If we don't believe, we could die like those that refused to cover their doorposts with the blood of the lamb during Passover.** The Holy Spirit is warning us to be ready and to be covered by the blood. To accept suffering for Christ as a badge of honor because God is trustworthy and he will do **everything** he promised he would do.

A PRAYER TO MOVE YOUR MOUNTAIN

Most Gracious and Heavenly Father,

We thank you for the opportunity to approach your throne in humility and praise. We glorify your all knowing presence and thank you for your love. Lord, we bless your holy and righteous name. Your Word says that we can do all things through you, who makes us strong. Right now, we pray for unwavering, walk on water faith to move mountains. Lord, we pray for open doors of favor and blessed relationships. We pray for intelligence and wisdom that specifically provides insight in areas of greatest need. Lord, we acknowledge that we must study to show ourselves approved and that we must forgive in order to be forgiven. Lord, right now we pray for your forgiveness and your mercy. Sometimes, we allow our desires to take hold of us and seep through us into a place of idol worship. Renew in us a clean heart and a right spirit that we may serve you in truth. God magnify and ignite our spiritual gifts. Help us to glorify your name through praise and worship. Help us to be content with the state we are in and help us to do what is right before your eyes with excellence. Lord, you are our refuge, our fortress, our shield and our exceeding great reward. You are our everything. Lord teach our hands, our minds and our spirits to war. Teach us to be strong on this battlefield. Help us to give of ourselves abundantly. Lord we believe as it reads in your Word (Luke 6:38), "Give and it shall be given to you pressed down, shaken together and running over through the hands of men will it come into your bosom." Help us to give Lord. Help us to give selflessly and to give as you instruct. We are blessed to be a blessing. We call on heaven to teach, reach and flow through us. Decrease us and increase you.

In Jesus Name We Pray, Amen.

Prophecy

"SURELY THE SOVEREIGN LORD DOES NOTHING WITHOUT REVEALING HIS PLAN TO HIS SERVANTS THE PROPHETS."
AMOS 3:7

In Context

The children of Israel were blessed by God. He had a special relationship with them. He saved them from slavery. In Amos 3, he warns them that destruction is coming because of their poor choices and behavior. He then uses metaphors to illustrate the power of prophecy. He calls for a prophet to warn Israel. God promises an adversary will bring down their power and that their land will be destroyed.

Destruction

God's power and authority are so great. He blesses and he curses. He gives and he takes. I remember a time when I'd just moved out of my sister's house and my little brother moved to live with me from Pennsylvania. I was telling him the story of Job. How Job lost everything but God restored double for his trouble. Within days of telling my brother that story a wind of destruction blew into my life. I lost my sales commission (I was promoted but made less as a result), I lost my financial aid, I totaled my car and before the year ended I filed for divorce. It was devastating. I felt like I'd lost it all. I couldn't believe how quickly everything changed.

"GO BACK AND TELL HEZEKIAH, THE RULER OF MY PEOPLE, 'THIS IS WHAT THE LORD, THE GOD OF YOUR FATHER DAVID, SAYS: I HAVE HEARD YOUR PRAYER AND SEEN YOUR TEARS; I WILL HEAL YOU. ON THE THIRD DAY FROM NOW YOU WILL GO UP TO THE TEMPLE OF THE LORD."
2 KINGS 20:5

In Context

King Hezekiah was sick and dying. The prophet Isaiah came to tell him that God desired he set his house in order because he would not live. Hezekiah cried and wept bitterly. He reminded God of his faithful service and his heart to obey. God stopped Isaiah in the courtyard outside of Hezekiah's home and had him return. The prophet told Hezekiah that God heard his prayers and agreed to allow him to live for 15 more years. He simply had to go up to the House of Lord three days from that day. Hezekiah asked for a sign to make sure this Word was indeed from God. When the sign was given, Hezekiah went to the House of the Lord and was healed. Soon after a prince approached Hezekiah for a visit. Hezekiah foolishly showed the man all his riches - everything he had. Isaiah arrived and asked Hezekiah, "Where are these men from?" Hezekiah told him that they were from Babylon and that he showed them his treasures. Then Isaiah prophesied, "Hear the Word of the Lord: Behold the days come that all in thine house, and that which thy fathers have laid up in store unto this day, shall be carried into Babylon, nothing shall be left saith the Lord." He even told him that his sons would be taken to become eunuchs in the palace of Babylon. Hezekiah, then responded, "Good is the Word of the Lord which thou has spoken. Is it not good if peace and truth be in my days?"

Final Notes

Abundance is not always financial. Sometimes it is being provided a supernatural insight into a situation that you cannot predict. God has blessed us with prophets within our midst. There was once a king that hated prophets and instead God sent a lying spirit to counsel him. While we make mistakes and the word God sends us may not always be good, we can always thank God because he at least gives us a warning of what is to come. In this lesson, he showed that we can even ask God for a different outcome. Without prophecy, Hezekiah would not have known to beg for his life.

A PRAYER TO MOVE YOUR MOUNTAIN

Most Gracious and Heavenly Father,

We thank you for the abundant gift of prophecy. We are so grateful that you think so wonderfully of us to provide warnings before anything transpires. Lord, we look to you for guidance. Please direct our path and make it straight, protect us, direct us and forgive us Lord for our shortcomings. We are not perfect but we love you and thank you for our lives. We thank you that you care enough about us to share a warning before something occurs. As long as we have you Lord, we don't need anyone or anything else. We are abundant with the Spirlt of Christ.

In Jesus Name, Amen.

Provision

"THE YOUNG LIONS DO LACK AND SUFFER HUNGER; BUT THEY WHO SEEK THE LORD SHALL NOT BE IN WANT OF ANY GOOD THING." PSALM 34:10

In Context
I will bless the Lord at all times! My soul will boast in the Lord. Bless the Lord with me. I cried to God and he heard me! He delivered me from every fear. His Angels surrounded me because I reverence him with the utmost respect. Taste and see that the Lord is good! Blessed is the man who trusts in him. The lions may search for food, but God's children lack no good thing. What man loves life and seeks good? He that watches his tongue and actions, and refrains from speaking evil or doing it. God turns his back on those that do evil. God's eyes are among the righteous and he hearkens when they cry. God is close to the broken hearted. Many are the afflictions of the righteous but the Lord delivers them from them all. The wicked are killed and the evil desolate but God saves his people.

Blessed to be a Blessing

I have been trying to get my bachelors degree for 10 years. All was going extremely well when I aggressively added an additional class during my senior year Spring semester. Financial aid wouldn't cover it. Nothing the school could do. I had to drop out and pay it back at slowly at $100 per month (all I could afford). After paying it back plus interest, 2 years had passed. One month after final payment, I reached out and enrolled. The degree I was seeking changed completely. At this rate, I would have to do four more years. I reached out to an advisor to see if anything could be done. She managed to get approval for most of my classes to be accepted and applied toward my degree. I was down to one year. I started taking classes while managing an aggressive local campaign. It was tough on me. I get to the last quarter, only three more classes. But, my financial aid ran out. I tried to pay out of pocket but failed. I emailed and called multiple advisors. Finally, I felt a nudging in my spirit to reach out to a dean at the school. He was no longer there but a new dean took his place. I sent the email to him. Soon after a hurricane hit my finances and I was facing possible homelessness, bills shut off notices and more. I never lost faith. A Christmas without one gift but I thanked God for Jesus Christ. It all slowly began to turn around. Two days ago I received a call from Regent University. It was the advisor the helped me adjust my degree plan. They heard about my hardships and agreed to pay the $3800 I owed and even what was necessary to finish. They congratulated me, I would walk on May 6, 2017! God is so amazing. All we have to do is just believe. He is going to make your wildest dreams come true if you just hold his hand in faith.

"FAITH IS THE SUBSTANCE OF THINGS HOPED FOR AND THE EVIDENCE OF THINGS UNSEEN." HEBREWS 11:1

In Context
Faith is believing beyond natural circumstance and embracing all that life can offer when you allow yourself to believe. Many of our biblical leaders excelled in life because they chose to believe and trust God. Abel brought his best to God and believed it was good enough. Enoch walked with God and defied death. Noah built an ark that saved his family. Abraham and his family's obedience allowed him to become the father of many nations. By faith, each sought the true promise of God. Isaac, Jacob, Joseph, Moses, Rahab, David... each heard the voice of God within their hearts and believed. In doing so, they offered powerful deliverance for God's people. In the same way, our faith will intertwine with their faith to produce more saved lives.

Final Notes
Abundance requires faith. We can't successfully fulfill the God-sized purpose he has placed in our hearts with feeble minded belief. We have

to step outside of what we see and even what we may be afraid of to embrace the beautiful possibilities God places in our hearts.

A PRAYER TO MOVE YOUR MOUNTAIN

Most Gracious and Heavenly Father,

Thank you for this beautiful moment with you. A time to hear your voice and grow in faith. Lord, we pray that you strengthen our faith to believe bigger, wider, 3D with Dolby Digital Sound size dreams. Eradicate our fears with an overflow of your spirit. We were created in your likeness to speak our dreams into existence. Regardless of what our abundant futures look like, we can't get there without your provision, direction and protection. Lord, we can't get there without faith. We humbly pray for an abundant spirit of faith that takes giant sized dreams from grasshopper perspectives and makes them a reality that not only changes our lives but powerfully changes the lives around us. Lord we openly admit that we believe! Yes, we trust you Lord to do exceedingly, abundantly more than we can ask, think or imagine.

In Jesus Name, Amen

Purpose

"SOW YOUR SEED IN THE MORNING, AND AT EVENING LET YOUR HANDS NOT BE IDLE, FOR YOU DO NOT KNOW WHICH WILL SUCCEED, WHETHER THIS OR THAT, OR WHETHER BOTH WILL DO EQUALLY WELL." ECCLESIASTES 11:3

In Context

Be generous, be a blessing to someone else, it yields great results. There are mysteries only God will know the answer to. Work hard from day until night, don't let time flow past you. Enjoy each day to the fullest, refusing to take one moment for granted. There will be many dark days which are smoke and mirrors of perceived darkness. A young person should enjoy their youth and chase dreams. Just remember God will hold you accountable for your decisions. Youth won't last always.

This or That

God has blessed me with many gifts. I can design. I can write. I can braid hair well. I have a strong passion for young people. Finally, I believe my purpose is to help others prepare for their next step in life. Whether it be through helping a small business develop great branding, preparing a press release for a company or offering leadership and etiquette to young people, I have found through pursuing many outlets that I love to give and live life as if I were a straight path for the Lord to travel and get to his people. I didn't know if design would get me the life I would love (when I pursued it I had no clue what life was about) but it allowed me to work for television stations, win national honors and work at a national magazine. I also didn't know if one person would ever read my books... or if it would be just me... But now I am booked to speak somewhere at least once a month. I didn't know if parents would trust me to help develop leadership and etiquette traits in their teens. Now I am hosting classes all over the nation and making an international impact. I never knew my life would flourish as a publicist allowing me to meet Danny Glover, Kevin Durant, Rickey Smiley, Tisha Campbell, Vivica Fox, Tyler Lepley, Al B. Sure, Serge Ibaka... let alone thrust me into politics. I just went for it.

"SEEST THOU A MAN DILIGENT IN HIS BUSINESS? HE SHALL STAND BEFORE KINGS; HE SHALL NOT STAND BEFORE ORDINARY MEN." PROVERBS 22:29

In Context
Choose integrity over greed; your reputation produces high esteem. The Lord made the rich and the poor. Don't ignore the problem or you will reap the consequences. True humility and

fear of God, lead to riches, honor and long life. Corruption leads to difficult roads. Teach your children in the way they should go and when they get old they will not depart from it. Just as the rich rule the poor, the borrower is slave to the lender. Being unjust will reap disaster. Generous people are blessed because they feed the poor. Throw out the mocker and fighting goes too. Whoever loves a pure heart and gracious speech will have the king as a friend. The Lord keeps those with knowledge and destroys the plans of the treacherous. The lazy let fear keep them from moving forward. The mouth of an immoral woman is a trap those that make the Lord angry fall into. Young people are foolish but physical discipline resolves that. Oppression of the poor for personal gain will result in poverty. The Lord is their defender and he will ruin anyone who ruins them. Stay away from hot-tempered people. Don't co-sign for anyone's debt, if you can't afford it your bed will be snatched from beneath you. Don't cheat your neighbor by moving former boundaries. A skilled man will serve kings and not ordinary people.

Final Notes

An abundant person recognizes their purpose as a tool in God's army. Often fitted with an armor of excellence this person will not limit his/her ability to serve to one option. Instead abundance requires you investigate and try a little of this or a little of that. As you grow in skill and the ability to identify your purpose, you will serve kings.

A PRAYER TO MOVE YOUR MOUNTAIN

Most Gracious and Heavenly Father,

We thank you for the power of your Holy Spirit that leads and guides us. We humbly bow before the throne of your grace with hearts of love. Lord, bless us with strategic opportunities that only you could create. Help us to serve in such a powerful way that our clients and employers are in awe at the gift you have anointed us with. Lord Jesus, as we serve people that are blessed with authority over us, help us to have a supernatural wisdom and discernment to guide, implement and provide strategic solutions to unique problems with mind blowingly positive results. Jesus, forgive us where we fall short. Boost our confidence, bless our families and those we serve.

In Jesus Name, Amen.

Protection

"THE LORD WILL FIGHT FOR YOU; YOU NEED ONLY TO BE STILL."
EXODUS 14:14

In Context

The Israelites just survived the first Passover and were freed from Egypt. As they left, God warned them to hide in a certain area because Pharaoh was going to change his mind. God hardened Pharaohs heart to show the Egyptians that he was God. Pharaoh chased after the Israelites with 600 of his best chariots and the remaining chariots throughout Egypt. The Israelites were afraid and began to complain. But, Moses assured them that God was on their side and all will be well. God was going to fight FOR them if they just waited. Then, it was time to move. Moses did as God commanded and raised his staff. The angels and God's pillar of smoke moved from in front of the Israelites to the rear, protecting them from Pharaohs army. As they approached the sea, it parted creating a hallway for the people of God to walk over to the other side. The ground they walked on was dry despite being created by two walls of water. Pharaohs army was in hot pursuit but God fought for them, twisting the wheels of the chariots. As soon as they reached the opposite side with Pharaohs chariots close behind, the walls of water descended and fell upon the army - swallowing them whole. When the Israelites saw this they were in awe. They trusted God and his servant Moses.

In the Nick of Time

Has God ever come to your rescue in the nick of time? He certainly has for me... time and time again. Once such time was prior to my daughter Dallas' graduation. I wanted desperately to make sure she had everything she needed before she went to the University of Central Oklahoma. In my heart, she needed a cell phone, a laptop and a car. A tall order I knew, but God planted that in my heart. I started by telling my family, maybe they could help... No, they couldn't. I was even told that if I thought that is what she needed, I should get it. With my single mom struggling check to check existence I assumed it was a disparaging comment. Well... the first thing I managed to get was the car! My aunt had just bought a new car. I went to see if she would take $600 for it. I could pay half now, half later. She said yes! It was a 2000 Cherry Red Pontiac Sunfire with tinted windows. A great graduation car, if you ask me. I couldn't give up. She'd gone get entire senior year without a cell phone and it was time to get another. I searched Craigslist but called AT&T first. I am glad I did. The person told me all kinds of horror stories. But, I was able to get her a phone with my credit. So, that's what I did! Now, my money was funny and my change was strange but I was down to the last of my budget and graduation was two days away. I searched Craigslist day and night. Made calls and haggled. I found one in the next county. Look at God! I arranged for her to be picked up by a friend so I could decorate her car. She has the most humble spirit and never complains. When we drove around the corner and saw the car she was practically speechless! I really surprised her. It was amazing what faith and trusting God could do.

"AS FOR GOD, HIS WAY IS PERFECT: THE WORD OF THE LORD IS TRIED: HE IS PROTECTION TO ALL THOSE THAT TRUST IN HIM."
PSALMS 18:30

In Context
I will love you Lord. You are my strength, my rock, my shield, my strong tower. I will put my trust in you. I will call on you and so shall I be saved from my enemies. Death haunted me and floods of ungodly men made me afraid. I cried out to God and he answered me. In fact the earth trembled at his anger. His nostrils flared as he flew on the wings of a cherub. Hail and fire followed his presence. He rescued me from my enemies that were too strong for me, they blocked me after

me fall but God restored me. He brought me into a large place because he delighted in me. The Lord blessed me according to my righteousness and according to my clean hands. Because I kept his ways and did not do evil. I meditated on his law day and night. God rewarded me. To those that show mercy he shows mercy. God will bless the afflicted and cast down the haughty looks. God's ways are perfect. His word is proven to be true. Who is a rock like our God? It is he that gives me strength and makes my way perfect. He has placed me in high places, he has made me strong, he has given me the shield of salvation and his gentleness has made me great. I have pursued my enemies and overtaken them, I chased them until they were consumed. I have wounded them that they were not able to rise. They cried but there was none to save them. You have made me head over heathen, people I don't know will serve me. Strangers will submit to me and those that simply hear my name will obey me. The Lord lives, blessed is my rock and the Lord of my salvation is to be praised! It is God that avenges me and subdues the people beneath me. He has delivered me from my enemies and has risen me above my enemies. Therefore I will give him praise among the heathen. He has delivered me and provided mercy, blessing the seed of David always.

Final Notes
You just can't beat having abundant protection!

No matter where we are in life, we are bound to face adversity. Sometimes, God allows it so that he can get the glory. Other times he is right there to defend, fight and protect you in every way. Abundance comes in many forms and we are abundantly blessed with his highest form of protection: salvation from death and the grave.

A PRAYER TO MOVE YOUR MOUNTAIN

Most Gracious and Heavenly Father,

Please forgive us for doubting your love in our toughest seasons of adversity. Help us to be still and trust that you are working on our behalf. When it is time to move, open our hearts and ears to hear your explicit instruction. Thank you for being our rock and shield. Thank you for allowing us to turn to you in our distress when we are surrounded by our enemies. Thank you for your unending love, mercy and grace. Thank you for the lavish and abundant gift of everlasting life and a promising eternity basking in your presence. You are flawless and your word is a beacon of light. Direct our path and make our way perfect.

In Jesus Name, Amen.

Faith

"THEREFORE I TELL YOU, WHATEVER YOU ASK FOR IN PRAYER,
BELIEVE THAT YOU HAVE RECEIVED IT, AND IT WILL BE YOURS."
MARK 11:24

In Context

Jesus sent two disciples ahead of him once they reached a certain city at the Mount of Olives. "Go into the city. You will find a colt that has never been ridden. Untie him and bring him here. If anyone asks why you do this, tell them the Lord has need of him," Jesus instructed. The disciples found the virgin colt in a place where two ways met (a crossroad) and loosed him. Someone nearby asked what they were doing and they responded as the Lord told them to. They brought the colt to Jesus and laid garments on him, then Jesus got on. They laid their garments and branches on the ground before him (making a straight way for the Lord to travel). All before and behind him cried aloud, "Hosanna, Blessed is he that comes in the name of the Lord. Blessed be the kingdom of our father, David that comes in the name of the Lord, Hosanna in the highest. Jesus entered into Jerusalem, observing and then onto Bethany, where he became hungry. He was happy to spot a fig tree where he might eat. But he was disappointed to see the tree looked like it was bearing fruit but actually was not. He cursed the tree for pretending to be something it wasn't. "No man will eat fruit from this tree forever." His disciples heard it. Then Jesus went into the temple and turned over the money changers and sellers of items for false idol worship. He also would not allow any man to carry a vessel through the temple. Then he said, "Is it not taught that my house shall be called a house of prayer by all nations? You have made it a den of thieves." Then he began knocking over the tables. The chief scribes and priests heard it. They were astonished by him and began to plot his destruction. Jesus left that evening and the next morning he and his disciples passed the fig tree without fruit. It was dead and leafless. Peter remarked, "Master the tree you cursed is dead and withered away."

Jesus was certain, "Have faith in God. For verily I say unto you, That whosoever shall say unto this mountain, Be thou removed, and be thou cast into the sea; and shall not doubt in his heart, but shall believe that those things which he saith shall come to pass; he shall have whatsoever he saith. Therefore I say unto you, What things soever ye desire, when ye pray, believe that ye receive them, and ye shall have them. And when ye stand praying, forgive, if ye have ought against any: that your Father also which is in heaven may forgive you your trespasses. But if ye do not forgive, neither will your Father which is in heaven forgive your trespasses." When Jesus returned to the temple the chief scribes and priests approached him questioning his authority. Jesus responded, "I will also ask of you one question, and answer me, and I will tell you by what authority I do these things. The baptism of John, was it from heaven, or of men? answer me." But they were afraid to answer because their logic would be questioned and considered negative either way. Instead they responded, we cannot tell. Then Jesus replied, "Neither do I tell you by what authority I do these things."

Abundant Faith

In 2016, I began the year believing that I would take the She's a BOSSE Etiquette Clinique to Atlanta. At first, I had no idea how I would do it. But as the year continued and I hadn't made any plans, I began to discredit my belief. I mean, I was the campaign manager for a candidate that faced great opposition. I wanted to focus because it was the opportunity of a lifetime. But, in my spirit, I felt God nudging me. Pushing me. So, I did it. I called and booked venues, a loft for the volunteers and I, restaurants for dining etiquette, photographers and speakers. Every time I paid a deposit, I prayed for God to make a way. I had to really work hard to make it happen. At the same time, God pushed me to finish my Bachelor's degree. But, again money was funny and change was strange. It was about a month and a half away and my bills were amounting to about $7,000... but I had faith that if God brought me to it, he would bring me through it. One morning as I worked, I heard a trash truck outside. Next thing I know, it sounded like they hit something or someone the way the man screamed. I looked out the window but didn't see anything. A couple of minutes later, he is knocking on my door. Turns out they hit my daughter's car that had been sitting outside my home for about 6 months at that point. Crazy. That became a settlement from the city for a good chunk of what was needed. (Mind you at the time I'd lost the keys to my Cadillac and was car less). Then, two weeks later, I got an unexpected financial aid check for close to the remainder of what was needed. I spent the last of my rent money paying the rest. The trip was excellent and the first time we served out of state with the brand. I was so grateful and amazed.

"AND WITHOUT FAITH IT IS IMPOSSIBLE TO PLEASE GOD, BECAUSE ANYONE WHO COMES TO HIM MUST BELIEVE THAT HE EXISTS AND THAT HE REWARDS THOSE WHO EARNESTLY SEEK HIM." HEBREWS 11:6

In Context

Faith is believing beyond natural circumstance and embracing all that life can offer through the eyes of faith. Many of our biblical leaders excelled in life because they chose to believe and trust God. Abel brought his best to God and believed it was good enough. Enoch walked with God and defied death. Noah built an ark that saved his family. Abraham and his family's obedience allowed him to become the father of many nations. By faith, each sought the true promise of God. Isaac, Jacob, Joseph, Moses, Rahab, David... each heard the voice of God within their hearts and believed. In doing so, they offered powerful deliverance for God's people. In the same way, our faith will intertwine with their faith to produce more saved lives. Without faith... it is impossible to please God and he rewards those that earnestly seek him.

Final Notes

Jesus knew that what God asked him to do would be difficult and life-threatening. In many ways, the things God will ask us to do will appear to be the same. Imagine, Noah building the ark amongst his peers and friends... they had to think he was crazy. Or what about Moses, who led a people away from their land to the end of the road... standing before a massive sea that seemingly walled them in to face their enemies. Or even me, who chose to pay for a conference in Atlanta instead of paying for my classes or a car – both I desperately needed. Or even what my candidate thought when a month before his most important election, a runoff, I had to go and serve this conference.... Life threatening faith is what God expects. He is faithful and you can trust him. But your faith in God has to be just as abundant as the gift he gives when he honors your faith before men. Abundant faith often requires abundant risk... and a little discomfort. But in the end, you will win.

A PRAYER TO MOVE YOUR MOUNTAIN

Most Gracious and Heavenly Father,

we thank you for the ability to come to you and ask what we will without judgement. We thank you for your sovereignty and presence in our lives. We thank you that you have sacrificed the most precious gift to save us – your life. We thank you for health and a sound mind. On this day, Lord, we ask for a double portion of your spirit to carefully discern what you would have us to do. Grant us supernatural faith and belief to do what seems impossible and to dream works bigger than our circumstance says we can do. We ask that you bless our coming and going. We ask that you bless our families, our places of business, our organizations, our futures and anoint each area with your Holy presence and direction. God give us strategic, life-giving, way-making communications, actions and insight to make a dramatic impact on the world around us. Help us to be your hands and feet in this earth. Direct our path and make it straight. God help us to see your will in every situation and to respond with childlike obedience – no matter what it looks like. Lord we trust you to not only protect us, but to direct us and to position us to serve with excellence. Open doors no man can shut and bless our coming and going. Lord Jesus, please anoint us to be a perfect conduit of your love, mercy and grace. Help us to share your message in a way that is relevant, soul searching, heart penetrating and effective. Lord, forgive us of our sins and where we fall short. Help us to remember that none is perfect, no not one. We thank you for abundant gifts, abundant faith, abundant protection, abundant provision, abundant prophecy. We thank you for abundance you give freely to those who trust you.

In Jesus Name, Amen.

Love

"LOVE MUST BE SINCERE. HATE WHAT IS EVIL;
CLING TO WHAT IS GOOD." ROMANS 12:9

In Context

To give your will and determination in the body over to God is a reasonable service and a beautiful sacrifice to God. Renew your mind rather than do as others in the world do. Then you can test and prove God's pleasing and perfect will. Be humble, not drunk with power or lust... but walk according to the faith God has instilled in you. We are all one body functioning together through Christ, each of us blessed with a different gift to serve. Operate in your gift. Don't fake love. Do it right and keep it real. Run from evil and stick to what is good. Honor your neighbor above yourself and be loyal to those that treat you well. Stay strong serving the Lord with powerful testimony, happy hope, patience in trial, faithful in prayer, great generosity and graceful hospitality. Bless and do not curse. Be happy for the happy and sad for the sad. Stay humble and be willing to associate with those of low position. No eye for an eye, do what you know is right before the world. Stay at peace with all people, let God get the revenge. God promises to repay and avenge. Instead feed, clothe and provide drink for your enemy. When you do, you will touch him deeply, overcome evil with good.

Love is an Action... Overcoming Evil with Good

When I was a little girl I was molested. As an adult, I was raped. I saw a man die right in front of me, he was murdered. I strongly believe one of my daughters was molested when she was young. I have been cheated on, lied to, deceived, betrayed... stomped on in every way. I am sure you have been hurt too. I don't believe that God allows us to experience pain or hurt or trauma because we deserve it or because he is trying to teach us some lessons. We may learn lessons in the process but I believe at the end of the day, he is trying to prove that love truly conquers all. Growing up, I didn't understand how to process all of the emotions, resentment and self-hatred I kept inside. Instead, I would have sex, over eat, or use drugs – all various forms of self-destruction. As I write, we are approaching Easter. I decided to do a 40-day liquid fast for my lent. But, last night, I caved. My body was so weak and honestly, I had an emotional day... one filled with rejection and questioning my choices and pain. I buckled. I prayed for God to forgive me and I ate my chicken sandwich! I am laughing but, I was also filled with guilt. How could I not sacrifice a meal when Christ sacrificed his life for me. I didn't feel conviction from God but I felt a strong sense of condemnation from the enemy. Here is the thing... God defeated death and sin a long time ago when he sent his son Jesus to die for us. It was the ultimate gift of abundant love. It was not a deficient or mediocre gift; not a 'I am going to wake you up, get you ready for school and kiss you on your way out the door love...' but an 'I am going to save you from the car wreck, help you overcome drug addiction, save your life from destruction and self-hate kind of love' you can't buy, google or find on a dating site. Love is an action. It is so real, it so volatile and so life giving that you can't change your mind about it. It is IN you. Once you run to Jesus, he never lets you go. So, while I (we) have experienced many unfair and painful hardships in this life... we are still breathing and still loved... because LOVE conquers all.

"DO UNTO OTHERS AS YOU WOULD HAVE THEM DO UNTO YOU."
LUKE 6:31

In Context

Jesus and his disciples were hungry and picking wheat during the Sabbath. The Pharisees asked, "Why are you doing such things on the Sabbath?" Jesus referenced a story of King David and the shew bread when he was on the run... he added that he was Lord of the Sabbath. On another occasion, he questioned the Jewish leaders whether it was better to do evil or good on the Sabbath. Afterward, he healed a man's hand. This infuriated the Pharisees and they began to plot against Jesus.

Jesus went to a mountain to pray. Afterward he spoke to his 12 disciples as a crowd of people arrived to listen and be healed. Jesus told them that the poor, hungry, distraught and rejected were actually blessed for eternity. In contrast, he also shared that the rich, well fed, well-spoken of and happy were temporary comforts. He explained that loving your enemies and treating them well, doing for them what you would have them to do for you was critical. Don't judge... or condemn but forgive that you may be forgiven. Give and others will give to you in abundance. The blind are unable to lead the blind lest both fall in a pit. No one is the teacher but those that are fully trained are like the teacher. No good tree bears bad fruit. A good man brings good things of the good stored up in his heart, for the mouth speaks what the heart is full of. It is the same with an evil man, they bring forth evil. Listen, why call on me if you aren't going to trust me? The man who believes me and does what I say has built his house on a rock that can withstand any storm. But the man that knows the word but refuses to practice it, will have his home blown away at the first storm and the destruction will be complete.

Final Notes

Love is an action that goes beyond doing good. Love is an action that starts in your heart. It flows through your thoughts, actions and words without really thinking about it. It is who you are. Some will consider you weak, but in reality your meekness is a reflection of the God living inside of you. You can rest at night knowing that God is working it out for your good. People will do and say all manner of evil about you just like they did Jesus. He was healing and teaching while the Pharisees were plotting and eventually planning his murder. Even one amongst his people betrayed him. But because he trusted God and walked in obedience, he got the last say. He is now Lord of Lord and King of Kings.

While we will never be Jesus, we are blessed when we walk in obedience as well. Allowing God to defend and staying in his perfect will. Remember, Love conquers all... this battle isn't ours, it's the Lord's.

A PRAYER TO MOVE YOUR MOUNTAIN

Most Gracious and Heavenly Father,

We thank you for the perfect gift of unending love. Lord, your love is so marvelous, so wonderful, so amazing... words can't express our gratitude. You are an awesome God. Lord, as we humbly bow before your presence in prayer, we ask for mercy, grace and love. Love to forgive our enemies, those that hurt us in the worst ways. Lord we pray for the power to love, to give, to stay humble and stay holy. It isn't easy for us to forgive ourselves for our poor choices or our intentional wrongs. Help us Lord. Lord, how abundant a gift is love when its power stretches far beyond what we see in the natural? It is something we aren't yet able to adequately define and Lord, we may never be able to define it. We pray that we embody what we do know, what you have taught us. That we are able to go out into a world that may not know you and be your hands and feet. That we are able to abundantly give love as we have abundantly received love. Agape love, Christ love, supernatural love that surpasses our understanding. Lord, help us to give this love to our families, to our children, to our coworkers, to our friends, to our clients, to our enemies. Lord, decrease us and increase you. Grant us supernatural wisdom and discernment to bless, to love and to do more than we could imagine we had the power to accomplish.

In Jesus Name, Amen.

Expectancy

"BUT BLESSED IS THE ONE WHO TRUSTS IN THE LORD,
WHOSE CONFIDENCE IS IN HIM." JEREMIAH 17:7

In Context

The sins of Israel are engraved on their hearts, and their spoil given away. Cursed is the man that trusts in men and whose heart has departed from the Lord. He will reside in dry places and not be able to recognize what is good. But blessed is the man that trusts in the Lord, whose confidence is in him. He will be like a tree planted by the water, with green leaves and no fear of drought, it will not cease to bring forth fruit. The Lord searches every man's heart and gives according to a man's ways. Just as a partridge sits on her eggs that will never hatch, a rich man that does not earn money in the right way will die a fool. The throne is your source for sanctuary. Those that deny it will be ashamed. Heal me Lord and I shall be healed, save me and I shall be saved. As you know, I have continued in the Word, speaking truth no matter the consequence.

Please don't terrorize me, you are my hope in a world of evil. Lord, please allow those that persecute me to be confounded and dismayed with double destruction but protect me. "Tell them this," says the Lord, "Honor the Sabbath day, doing no work... not even in your home. If you honor the Sabbath, praising God with sacrifice, your city shall remain forever. If not, I will destroy the palaces of Jerusalem, it shall not be quenched.

Trusting God... and Praying for Deliverance

It may sound absolutely crazy but an alcoholic strengthened my faith and helped me to truly see God. When I was in my late twenties, I partied hard. I lived in Atlanta as a single beautiful mother of two and I think I could get anything I wanted if I batted my eyes and wore the right pair of jeans. Well, the cost of living was high and my lifestyle was expensive. I always wanted the best. I remember sitting in the studio with friends getting "uplifted" and complaining about my stacking bills. A woman that was there, an alcoholic, asked me, "Where is your faith?" I asked her what she meant and she went on to tell the story about her dreams and how God helped her to make them come true. She attributed it all to faith. Well, as time went on things went from bad to worse as I began to use cocaine. This caused me great distress and was beginning to affect my work performance... let alone being a mother. Then, I totaled another car... I believe it was the 4th, 5th or 6th one that year. I was stranded with nowhere to go and no one to help me. I turned to God and began to confess my faith as I learned it.

That one conversation changed my entire life. I have never been able to thank my friend, but trust me... I owe her the biggest hug! God knew exactly what I needed to hear and knew it was the right time for me to hear it. Having faith and placing all my confidence in God and not what I see, hear or even imagine is what carries me from day to day. I love God and I am so grateful I can trust him to see me through. In fact, he is not only helping me to survive, he is pushing me to thrive!

"BUT REMEMBER THE LORD YOUR GOD,
FOR IT IS HE WHO GIVES YOU THE ABILITY TO PRODUCE
WEALTH, AND SO CONFIRMS HIS COVENANT, WHICH HE SWORE
TO YOUR ANCESTORS, AS IT IS TODAY." DEUTERONOMY 8:18

In Context

Do exactly as I instruct so that you are able to enter your promised land. Remember how the Lord your God led you through the wilderness to humble and test you in order to know what was in your heart and if you could be obedient. He humbled you, when you were hungry it was he that fed you... not your work, to teach you that man does not live on bread alone but on every word that comes from the mouth of the Lord.

You were safe, and just as you discipline your kids, the Lord your God disciplines you. Walk in obedience to God and revering him. Because God is bringing you into your promised land where bread will not be scarce and you will lack nothing. When you have eaten and are satisfied, praise the Lord your God for the good land he has given you. Do not forget the Lord and become disobedient. Or after you have been blessed in your heart will become proud and you will forget the Lord, who saved you. He led you through the haters and booby traps and fed you when you couldn't feed yourself so that in the end it might go well for you. If you think to say, "My power and the strength of my hands have produced this wealth for me." Remember God, for it is he who gives you the ability to produce wealth, and in doing so keeps his promise made to your ancestors long ago. If you ever forget the Lord and follow other gods and worship and bow down to them, I testify against you today that you will surely be destroyed. Like the nations the Lord destroyed before you, so you will be destroyed for not obeying the Lord your God.

Final Notes

One thing we can count on is the Word of God will always be true. We can place abundant expectancy in God's faithfulness. In the Bible, God has given us the answers to the test, all we have to do is walk in obedience. We all remember a time when we were struggling... some of us are struggling as we read this. If you are struggling or have struggled, it is God allowing you to understand that he is God, that he is faithful and that it is he that has the power to elevate you or destroy you. Let us all be sober and thankful that we can fully expect God to be faithful and true to his word. As we journey into our promised lands, we must engrave these acknowledgments into our hearts and minds that they may show in our actions, beliefs and confessions.

A PRAYER TO MOVE YOUR MOUNTAIN

Most Gracious and Heavenly Father,

We thank you for the precious gift of abundant expectancy. We can stand on your Word as a firm foundation and rock of excellence. Lord, as we journey in our day to day lives reaping the benefit of calling you Father, help us to keep you and your will first. Help us to be obedient to you despite circumstance or opinion. Help us to be real followers of faith, developing a relationship with you that is bigger and better than we can even imagine. Your love for us is infinite, let our gratitude and loyalty to you reflect that we appreciate it. Lord, we know, we confess and we expect you to shower us with unending blessings and bring us out of any troubled water. Help us to remember you, to honor you and to bless your Holy Name. We accept and recognize that we are nothing without you. Decrease us and increase you. Lead us and help us to be all that you have created us to be.

In Jesus Name, Amen.

Open Doors

"THUS SAYS THE LORD TO CYRUS HIS ANOINTED,
WHOM I HAVE TAKEN BY THE RIGHT HAND, TO SUBDUE NATIONS
BEFORE HIM AND TO LOOSE THE LOINS OF KINGS; TO OPEN
DOORS BEFORE HIM SO THAT GATES WILL NOT BE SHUT."
ISAIAH 45: 1

In Context

God anointed and appointed Cyrus to get people
in line. He not only placed his hand upon him,
but he also opened doors and went before him
that no one could come against him. He wanted
the people to know that it was indeed God that
had called him, protects him and directs him to
do his work. That he was chosen by God. As he
explained this to Cyrus, he shared, "You don't
even know me! I am God, the ONLY God there
is. Besides me there are no real gods. I am the
one who armed you for this work. That the world
may know that there is no God beside me." As
creator of heaven and earth, God pronounced
doom on anyone who fights him. Would a child
fight a parent that gave them life? He reiterates
that it is he that made all things in the earth and

the earth itself. Then he shares, I chose Cyrus to do this. He will rebuild my cities. I didn't hire him, I told him to do it. The oppressors will flow to you freely, in chains, doing your will as I have commanded it. The creators of false idols will bury their heads in shame. God created the earth for a purpose, not for riff raff to ruin it all and to leave it empty. No it is to be lived in. I am the only God who knows and does what is right. Those others pray to a dead stick. I am the only God there is, the only one who does things right. Every word out of my mouth does what it says. I never take back what I say. All who rage against God will be brought low in disgrace, but those that are connected to him will have a robust, praising, good life in God!

Shouting for the Victory

Have you ever been in a battle that seemed unwinnable? The odds were stacked against you but somehow... you made it? Well, I know you have read about my victory in education with my school being paid for, victory in ministry with an Atlanta conference being paid for... but today, I will tell you about a season of walking to and from place to place after sacrificing to help a friend. As a business owner with bad credit, it was difficult for me to get a new car and a seemingly insurmountable task.

By the end of 2015, I decided I would serve one client, predominantly. I took on additional work but it was simply design projects, nothing comprehensive or time consuming. As a result, it was difficult to pay my bills. I still stayed committed to see this bigger project through and to do a great job. I did. But, by May of 2016, my full coverage insurance lapsed and I ended up rear ending a young lady on my way to see the last airing of "Purple Rain" at the downtown Harkins Theatre (after a long day of work). I had a co-worker in the car with me that insisted I stop and let him get a beer. I erroneously assumed he would open it in the dark theatre but was surprised he opened it IN MY CAR. As I looked over at him in shock, I rear ended a young lady in an SUV headed to her senior prom. This began a season of difficulty I can't describe as things I took for granted became extremely difficult, grocery store trips, visiting family or friends, even paying bills.

I fell into a depression when my work ended and income dried up. I was still without a car or resolution. I was dedicated to continue all of the annual projects and philanthropy work I did every year including leadership and etiquette programs for teens and women. I even managed to do the Atlanta trip without a car! These are definitely feats I could only do with God.

By the end of 2016, I determined I would use my tax dollars on a new used car. But, I attended a New Year's Eve party – A prayer party that I had to get to. I walked two miles to get there, in the cold December weather. It was an amazing evening and a lot of fun, strategic prayer and developed friendships. One of my friends asked about an annual event I do (which I'd already decided I just couldn't afford to do – times had been so difficult). But, to be honest, I'd already thought about what I would do if I did it. So when she asked, I just blurted it out. "Yes, we are taking that program to Dallas, are you coming with me?" It was funny. So, I thought, I guess I am giving those tax dollars to KYSE. But, by the end of January, I found out the monies wouldn't come in time! I panicked. But, I knew it was an assignment from God and what he leads you to, he will get you through. I got through it and it was marvelous! I made exactly what I needed to make to get it done.

I received my income tax refund and set out to find the perfect used car. I wanted a BMW. Every car I looked at was a lemon. I began to get hopeless. A friend that blessed me to take me to get the car told me to go to a dealership. But, the way the last 12 months had gone, I was nervous. She looked at me and said, "Don't be scared." I smiled. We went from lot to lot looking for the perfect vehicle. I'd told her my plans to purchase a small used car I could give to my youngest daughter and to later get an SUV for the programs. We found a 2007 BMW X5. A combination of both dreams. It was a beautiful car but I was intimidated. But, God did it. He worked it out. I am so happy.

"AND TO THE ANGEL OF THE CHURCH IN PHILADELPHIA WRITE: HE WHO IS HOLY, WHO IS TRUE, WHO HAS THE KEY OF DAVID, WHO OPENS AND NO ONE WILL SHUT, AND WHO SHUTS AND NO ONE OPENS, SAYS THIS: 'I KNOW YOUR DEEDS BEHOLD, I HAVE PUT BEFORE YOU AN OPEN DOOR WHICH NO ONE CAN SHUT, BECAUSE YOU HAVE A LITTLE POWER, AND HAVE KEPT MY WORD, AND HAVE NOT DENIED MY NAME." REVELATIONS 3:7-8

In Context

In Revelations 3, a letter is written to each of the churches in Sardis, Philadelphia and Laodicea. To Sardis, God warns: I see you working but not for me. I know that you are busy but you are focused in the wrong direction. Return to what you heard originally and work in your purpose. You will not know when I am coming, repent. To Philadelphia, He assures: I open doors no man can open and shut doors no man can shut. I have seen you working hard to keep my word. Even when it was hard for you, you still believed. You have little strength but you have held on. You have not denied my name. There are many that call themselves righteous but aren't being real. Hold on to your crown tightly and don't allow distractions to pull you away. When all is said and done, I will exalt you before them and all will know who really worshipped me in wholeness and truth. To Laodicea, God warns: Get it together. You teeter totter between good and evil but it would be much better if you make a choice to be one or the other. trust me. I will make you white as snow and ensure that shame does not befall you. I am here because I love you and I want the best for you. Listen, I am standing at the door knocking. If you let me in, I will come in and eat with you. At my table, I sit among conquerors... Because only conquerors sit at the table in a place of honor. Just as I have conquered and sit at the side of my Father. His disciples tell him he is blessed as they bring him to Jesus. The man, overjoyed rushed over. Jesus asked, "What can I do?" The man responded, "Teacher, I would like to see." Jesus responded, "Go, your faith has made you well." He was instantly given sight and followed Jesus down the road.

Final Notes

The Lord is a strong tower and the righteous run in to be saved. In this lesson, God is saying the opposite. He is saying, I am sending you to fight for and defend the honor of God. But not only am I sending you, but I have my hand on you, I have the door wide open, I have already gone before you. God is sending you to a place where you can do his will in peace without worry of shame. Don't concern yourself with the enemies that possess the land now, go forward in faith. God has already blessed this place and you to do his will and redeem his land. It is time for you to sit at the table with conquerors. Have faith.

A PRAYER TO MOVE YOUR MOUNTAIN

Most Gracious and Heavenly Father,

There is power in your name. As we take the time to call on you in our times of need for direction, protection and alignment of our will with your purpose, strengthen our faith. We dare not question the assignment, instead we believe, we move and we conquer the lands you are sending us to. Help us to be worthy ambassadors choosing your will above our own. Help us to share your message and your love in a way that is not only compelling but life changing. Lord help us to be all that you have created us to be. Help us to trust the firm foundation of your Word. Help us to reap where we have not sown, to live where we have not built, to conquer lands with excellence and to bring you glory. Forgive us of our sins, where we fall short and help us to return to you. Give us humble, submissive spirits that we may hear those beautiful words when we return, "Well Done, Good and Faithful Servant."

In Jesus Name, Amen.

Giving

"BUT WHEN YOU GIVE TO THE NEEDY, DO NOT LET YOUR LEFT HAND KNOW WHAT YOUR RIGHT HAND IS DOING, SO THAT YOUR GIVING MAY BE IN SECRET. THEN YOUR FATHER, WHO SEES WHAT IS DONE IN SECRET, WILL REWARD YOU.' MATTHEW 6:4

In Context

Don't do it for applause, people may clap but God isn't. "When you do something for someone else, don't call attention to yourself. Helping people is something you should do behind the scenes. Praying for an audience is wrong as well, God is watching but he isn't impressed. Instead, find a quiet, secluded place so you won't be tempted to pretend before God. Shift your thinking from you to God that you will experience his grace. The world is full of so-called prayer warriors peddling techniques for getting what you want from God. Don't drink the koolaid. The Father knows better than you what you need. With a God like this loving you, you can pray very simply. Like this: Our Father in heaven, hallowed is your name, your kingdom come, your will be done, as it is in heaven, as it is in earth, give us this day, our daily bread, forgive us our debts, as we forgive our debtors, lead us not into temptation and deliver us from evil, for yours is the kingdom, and the glory, forever and ever. Amen. In prayer there is a connection between what God does and what you do. You must forgive to be forgiven. God is a reactionary God, he responds to your actions. Fast in secret. Look normal, act normal knowing that God sees and hears. Don't try to impress people, impress God. Rather than save your treasure on earth (where it can easily get stolen) build it in heaven, where it's safe from destruction and theives. What you treasure is where you will be. Your eyes are windows into your body. Open your eyes, see the good that God brings... but if you are distrustful and hard eyed, you will live a dismal life. You can't worship two gods at once. Loving one god, you'll end up hating the other. Adoration of one feeds contempt for the other. You can't worship God and Money both. Choosing a life with God means that what you wear and eat are not concerns, just as God takes care of the birds, he will take care of you. Relax, do not be so preoccupied with getting, so you can respond to God's giving. Choose God over everything and he will be sure to take care of you. Give your entire attention to what God is doing right now, and don't get worked up about what may or may not happen tomorrow. God will help you deal with whatever hard things come up when the time comes.

Extravagant Blessings

Earlier in the book, I discussed being surprised and getting a full scholarship to finish my bachelor's degree. Well, what you don't know is that two days before, I resolved that if God didn't need me to have a degree to do what he created me to do, I was fine with it. I felt like a degree at that point may have just been a selfish desire. Then, one day after that, but one day before I received the call about the scholarship, one of the KYSE girls that couldn't go on the trip I'd been helping (unbeknownst to anyone except a local pastor I asked to pray and another woman that I thought could help her get hired) was struggling. When she was nominated for the program her fiancé revealed why she was struggling with her self-esteem (job loss and an accident that caused her to lose her two front teeth, making it difficult for her to have confidence). I felt like my only responsibility was to help her strengthen her faith in God, confessing and believing and trusting him. So, anyway, she ended up not going on our trip because she was called for a second interview. When we returned, we continued conversations (today she has a job!) but before she got it, I revamped her resume, prayed with her before interviews and helped her to get a set of cosmetic teeth (affordable online set with excellent reviews). The day after I surprised her with a gift card to order the teeth she told me about (mind you, I just purchased a new car and was literally down to my last) ... God sent word that I received a more than 7k scholarship to finish school. This scripture, about working in secret, blessed in the open is no joke. You can trust God and you don't need the accolades from people when the creator of the universe is impressed with your abundant thinking to give and love on others.

"GIVE, AND IT SHALL BE GIVEN UNTO YOU; GOOD MEASURE, PRESSED DOWN, AND SHAKEN TOGETHER, AND RUNNING OVER, SHALL MEN GIVE INTO YOUR BOSOM. FOR WITH THE SAME MEASURE THAT YE METE WITHAL IT SHALL BE MEASURED TO YOU AGAIN." LUKE 6:8

In Context

Jesus and his disciples were hungry and picking wheat during the Sabbath. The Pharisees asked, "Why are you doing such things on the Sabbath?" Jesus referenced a story of King David and the shew bread when he was on the run... he added that he was Lord of the Sabbath. On another occasion, he questioned the Jewish leaders whether it was better to do evil or good on the Sabbath. Afterward, he healed a man's hand. This infuriated the Pharisees and they began to plot against Jesus.

Jesus went to a mountain to pray. Afterward he spoke to his 12 disciples as a crowd of people arrived to listen and be healed. Jesus told them that the poor, hungry, distraught and rejected were actually blessed for eternity. In contrast, he also shared that the rich, well fed, well-spoken of and happy were temporary comforts. He explained that loving your enemies and treating them well, doing for them what you would have them to do for you was critical. Don't judge... or condemn but forgive that you may be forgiven. Give and others will give to you in abundance. The blind are unable to lead the blind lest both fall in a pit. No one is the teacher but those that are fully trained are like the teacher. No good tree bears bad fruit. A good man brings good things of the good stored up in his heart, for the mouth speaks what the heart is full of. It is the same with an evil man, they bring forth evil. Listen, why call on me if you aren't going to trust me? The man who believes me and does what I say has built his house on a rock that can withstand any storm. But the man that knows the word but refuses to practice it, will have his home blown away at the first storm and the destruction will be complete.

Final Notes
Jesus sees you and what you do. You don't have to sound the alarm. You don't have to cry out for others to see your sacrifice, whether it be gift, fasting, praying or other. You are worshipping a God that can see, and you will know he sees you by his reaction. Don't spend your life chasing things that don't have value. God gives abundantly to those who give of themselves to

himself abundantly. Abundance is provided when God can see that you trust him enough to obey him, to love him, to honor him in public and to be in a real relationship with him. He wants to be your best friend.

A PRAYER TO MOVE YOUR MOUNTAIN

Most Gracious and Heavenly Father,

Thank you for desiring to be our friend. While we are rejected by many, to be loved by the creator of all things is truly enough. Lord, we know that we don't have to sound an alarm when we do good things to get men to love us. All we need to do is trust you. Help us to trust you Lord. Help us to obey you. Help us to sacrifice, pray and be in relationship with you in secret. Help us to obey you immediately, help us to run to your purpose in our lives. Give us the strategies, the methods, the gifts we need in order to be not only effective God, but supernaturally real and authentic. Showing that you are the head of our lives, nothing and no one else. Lord, remove fear. Defeat the enemy. Let no weapon that is formed against us prosper. Please encamp your angels of protection around us and our families. Help us to be role models to our family, showing what a life with Jesus can do. Help us to be everything you created us to be. Help us to love you more than anything we desire in this life: money, cars, relationship, fame, power – help us to hunger and thirst for more of you each day. Lord, as we walk, we know that we are not perfect. Help us to walk with a clean heart and a right spirit. Forgive us of our sins and help us to forgive those that have sinned against us. We honor you, we love you, we adore you.

In Jesus Name, Amen

Tithing

"AND HE BLESSED HIM AND SAID, "BLESSED BE ABRAM BY GOD MOST HIGH, POSSESSOR OF HEAVEN AND EARTH; AND BLESSED BE GOD MOST HIGH, WHO HAS DELIVERED YOUR ENEMIES INTO YOUR HAND!" AND ABRAM GAVE HIM A TENTH OF EVERYTHING.'
GENESIS 14:19-20

In Context

In Genesis 13, Abram and his nephew parted ways. Lot headed toward Sodom (greener pastures) and Abram the opposite direction. God promised Abram in that moment that everything he could see would belong to he and his descendants. In Genesis 14, several kings are at war. The war went on and on eventually warriors ended up facing each other in formation in the Valley of Siddim, which was full of tar pits. When the kings of Sodom and Gomorrah ran, they fell into a tar pit, but the other kings with them got away. The opposing armies looted all they had and left. They also captured Lot, Abram's nephew and took everything he owned. A fugitive got word of it to his uncle, Abram. Abram gathered all 318 of his servants (born in his household) and chased those that captured Lot all the way to Dan. They split into small groups and attacked, recovering everything the enemy took while rescuing Lot and the others. After Abram rescued them, Melchizedek, king of Salem, brought out bread and wine, he was the priest of the Most High God, and blessed him. He told him that he was blessed by the Most High God, the creator of Heaven and Earth, and blessed be the Most High God, who handed your enemies over to you. In response, Abram rendered one tenth of all he recovered. The king of Sodom asked for his people but told Abram he could keep the goods. But Abram told him, "I swear to God, The High God, Creator of Heaven and Earth, this solemn oath, that I'll take nothing from you, not so much as a thread or a shoestring. I'm not going to have you go around saying, 'I made Abram rich.' Nothing for me other than what the young men ate and the share of the men who went with me, Aner, Eschol, and Mamre; they're to get their share of the plunder."

Gratitude and Loyalty

We all have a clear sense of what it is like to hear the words, "Thank you." We love and appreciate when we are loved and appreciated! However, we sometimes forget that loyalty is just as important. When we are disloyal, it hurts those that have served us with greatness, honesty, commitment and trust. It breaks a bond that may not have been spoken but was thought to be understood.

I have always been a great helper to many. If it is in my power to do, I will do it. From opening my home to those that may be homeless, to serving in ways that aren't required. At one time, I helped one of our KYSE women get a job with a prominent company. The owner was also my client. Once inside this place of business and seeing the amount of money that came in, the prestige with being associated and the honor bestowed when doing a good job, it became her intention to sway the client from working with me. I cannot for any good reason consider why she thought this was a good idea, except to increase her personal gain (which in the end it did). But, it also broke my heart. I considered her a friend and had done so many great things for she and her child. It hurt me to the core. But, I had to learn that all people won't reciprocate, be loyal or say thank you. The client hurt me greatly as well, because I did serve with excellence... but it was worse coming from someone I opened many doors for. In this lesson, Abram remained loyal to God in the face of becoming rich... he chose to walk with God who he trusted to keep his promise. He was not only grateful, he was loyal.

"FOR THIS MELCHIZEDEK, KING OF SALEM, PRIEST OF THE MOST HIGH GOD, MET ABRAHAM RETURNING FROM THE SLAUGHTER OF THE KINGS AND BLESSED HIM, AND TO HIM ABRAHAM APPORTIONED A TENTH PART OF EVERYTHING. HE IS FIRST, BY TRANSLATION OF HIS NAME, KING OF RIGHTEOUSNESS, AND THEN HE IS ALSO KING OF SALEM, THAT IS, KING OF PEACE."
HEBREWS 7:1-2

In Context
The New Testament book of Hebrew, Chapter 7 brings clarity to who Melchizedek truly represents. Melchizedek (his name means righteousness) was the king of Salem (which means peace). In this way, the writer of Hebrews connects Melchizedek as an Old Testament reflection of Jesus. Abraham's tithe to Melchizedek was in response to the law that required priests that are descendants of Levi to collect a tithe. Most of the priests and people were in some way related to Abraham, but Melchizedek wasn't. In fact, he was a complete stranger that not only collected tithes but also pronounced a blessing. A blessing can only come from a greater person. Most priests die, but by giving his tithe to Melchizedek, he is recognized as giving it to a priest who "lives" (Jesus) and since the Levites are descendants of Abraham, when we pay our tithes, we too are giving back to Melchizedek in honor of the Most High God who lives.

Final Notes
Gratitude and loyalty to God is the highest praise we can give. Loyalty may mean giving up instant riches to do what is right before God even when it is not impressive or popular. When you trust God, like Abraham did, you don't look for the praise of people, you rest in the promise of God. Tithing is only one tenth of the wonderful gifts God has given us. To pay tithe to our local church, is in fact, giving it to God and not the messenger. If we

begin to see our gifts to God as a holy sacrifice to Christ himself (and not those collecting it), we are telling God thank you and we trust you.

A PRAYER TO MOVE YOUR MOUNTAIN

Dear Lord,

You are an awesome God. We thank you for the ability to tithe and to say thank you. We are grateful to have a God so wonderful and great to be loyal to. You open doors no man can shut, you close doors no man can open. You protect us from dangers seen and unseen. You promised that no weapon formed against us shall prosper. You are our solid rock on which we can always stand. As we journey this earth and are offered so many great and wonderful gifts, help us to see you in every situation. Help us to recognize your gift, the sacrifice you made on the cross to be Emmanuel, God with us is more precious than our tithe. Lord, you promised us that if we bring our tithes into the storehouse that you would open the windows of heaven and pour us out a blessing that is too big to receive. How awesome it is to say thank you and be rewarded with an even greater promise! You are an abundant God that offers abundant blessings. Lord, help us to be more like Abraham, trusting in your promises by faith. Help us to remain grateful and loyal to you, help us to trust you Lord. You are our rock, our shield and our greatest reward. Lord, you know what we stand in need of before we even ask, so we pray that you continue to walk with us, talk with us, lead us and protect us. We ask that you grant us a supernatural and strategic abundance of wisdom and discernment concerning our spiritual relationship with you, our health, our finance, our emotional and mental state, our businesses, our families. Lord, we know you are going to bless us. We thank you and we humbly ask that if there is anything in us that is not like you that you remove it. Decrease us and increase you. Forgive us of our sins.

In Jesus Name, Amen.

Investing

"PLANS FAIL FOR LACK OF COUNSEL, BUT WITH MANY ADVISERS THEY SUCCEED." PROVERBS 15:22

In Context

Wisdom waits to speak and searches for the right answer while doing good, evil refuses knowledge and desires a poor path that leads to trouble. The LORD pays attention to all things, both the evil and the good. Better to have little, with fear for the LORD, than to have great treasure and inner turmoil. Plans go wrong for lack of advice; many advisers bring success. Everyone enjoys a fitting reply; it is wonderful to say the right thing at the right time! A cheerful look brings joy to the heart; good news makes for good health. If you listen to constructive criticism, you will be at home among the wise. If you reject discipline, you only harm yourself; but if you listen to correction, you grow in understanding. Fear of the LORD teaches wisdom; humility precedes honor.

A Fool for Gluttony

When I was a teenager, my mom would send me out on cold winter mornings to start her car. I really wanted to learn to drive. So each morning, while I knew she wasn't paying attention, I would drive her car around the block. One morning it was especially cold and the roads iced over. But, I couldn't help indulging in my hidden treasure. I remember slowly backing the car out of the driveway and easing it up the street. Within minutes, the car began to slip and slide on the icy road... I knew I was in too deep. But I was committed to seeing it through. I'd almost made it around the block when suddenly, the car was stuck on a patch of ice. I knew it was game over and my mom (who doesn't play) was going to kill me. A friendly man in a van volunteered to help me get the car out by nudging my moms car forward with his bumper. It sounded like a great idea. I got in, put the car in neutral and waited for his gentle push. Instead, I hear a loud crunch. He ruined my mom's tail lights and the car hadn't moved an inch. My panic subsided in a waterfall of tears. It was ridiculous. I knew better. But, I allowed my emotions to dictate my fate. I had no choice but to face the wrath of my mother and it was going to hurt. Doing things my way caused me to get in a lot of trouble and cost my mom repairs. I should have just asked her to teach me...

In Context

Evil people plot violence and their hearts stir up trouble. Don't desire their company. A house built upon wisdom becomes strong based on good sense. The wise are mightier than the strong and those with knowledge grow stronger and stronger. Don't go to war without wise guidance; victory depends on having many advisers. Fools have nothing to say amongst leaders, troublemakers are known for evil. If you fail under pressure, you lack strength. Rescue those that are unjustly sentenced to die – God sees all hearts and he will repay. If you find wisdom you will have a bright future. Don't plot evil against the godly, they may fall seven times but one fall can overthrow evil people. Don't rejoice when your enemies fall, God may be displeased with you. Don't be jealous of evil people, they have no future. Don't associate with rebels, disaster will hit them suddenly. Don't show favoritism, judge justly. An honest answer is like a kiss of friendship. Plan and prepare before you build. Don't lie without cause, to get revenge. The lazy are recognized by their yard, overgrown and uncared for. Work hard.

Final Notes

The best investments are made in wisdom, good

advice, hard work, godly nature and right speech. These will lead you to an abundant life and are worthwhile investments.

A PRAYER TO MOVE YOUR MOUNTAIN

Most Gracious and Heavenly Father,

We thank you for the gift of wisdom and it's application of knowledge. Lord, open our hearts and minds to receive your direction, correction and protection. Help us to do your will, in speech, deed and thought. Help us to choose godly friends and to entrust our plans to the right circle that they may advise us with excellence. Lord, thank you for sending increase. Help us to help others, especially those in trouble. Lord, teach us to work hard and with excellent craftsmanship and skill. Grant us a supernatural insight and wisdom that surpasses understanding but is strategically guided by your excellent word. Lord we thank you for your sacrifice on the cross that allows the Holy Spirit to convict when we are wrong. Please forgive us of our sins, decrease us and increase you.

In Jesus Name, Amen.

Saving

"FOR WHICH OF YOU, INTENDING TO BUILD A TOWER, SITTETH NOT DOWN FIRST, AND COUNTETH THE COST, WHETHER HE HAVE SUFFICIENT TO FINISH IT?" LUKE 14:28

In Context

One Sabbath, Jesus had dinner with Pharisee and Saducee leadership. Everyone was watching them. He asked them if It was lawful to heal on the Sabbath, then he stood up and healed a man. He turned and asked everyone if any of them would leave a child or animal that fell into a well on the Sabbath without rescue. He then, noticing that some of the men at his table were fighting for prime seating, taught them a principle of humility. Instead of putting yourself in a place of honor, you are to allow someone else to invite you to the place of honor. Not only will you be the talk of the room, but you will be esteemed. Then he instructed the host, don't just invite your well to do friends, invite those that can never repay and who would appreciate the meal. In doing so, the host would be invited to sit at God's dinner table. Then he told a story about a man that created an elaborate celebration. He invited all of the upper echelon but each of them made excuses as to why they could not attend. He then sent his servants to find people hungry in the streets and those on the countryside. He refused to have an empty house and he refused to allow those that turned him away to enter his celebration.   One day, a large group walked with Jesus. "Anyone who comes to me must be able to let go of it all. Walk away from family and greatest desires. If you can't do that, you can't be my disciple," he said. Then he asked, "What man builds a house without first figuring the cost, people whisper about him starting a thing but not being able to finish it. Or what about a king, not prepared for battle? Won't he search the matter and ask for a truce if he knows he is unable to win?"   In order to walk with Christ, you must turn away – plans and people, to follow God. Salt is excellent. But if it goes flat, it's useless and good for nothing. Are you listening, really listening?

Leaving it all

In 2011, I left it all: my marriage, my newly purchased dream house, my stable job. I left it all in Atlanta, because I heard God calling me to Washington, DC. I did it. I left it all. It wasn't easy and my family and friends thought I was crazy. When I got to DC. My daughters and I were basically homeless. I had about 10K in 401K funds which I depleted within three months. From food, to car payments, phone bill and $1k rent, we were lucky to survive that long. While I stayed in faith, prayed and looked for a job. Nothing appeared. I was hopeless and homeless. But... I trusted God. I mean... I did what he told me to do. So, why did this happen. I look back and I think it was a test. Plus, it brought me back to Oklahoma which was a miracle. I almost vowed never to return. I am glad I did. This is my promised land. The place where God has blessed me most. The cost of living is great, I have a ton of family here and my business is doing well. God had and has a very strategic plan for my life. I trust him. If he asked me to leave it all today (a scary thought), I would. Because I do trust him. I hope and pray that he doesn't ask me to do that because I do love my life. But, I don't love it more than I love him, because without a doubt... I know he loves me.

"A GOOD MAN LEAVES AN INHERITANCE TO HIS CHILDREN'S CHILDREN, BUT THE SINNER'S WEALTH IS LAID UP FOR THE RIGHTEOUS." PROVERBS 13:22

In Context
Intelligent children listen to their parents. Good people love helpful conversation and careful words make for a careful life. The lazy want it all but get nothing. A good person hates lies. Loyalty to God will keep you on the right path. A fashion show life is empty. The rich get sued, the poor are free. God shines a light on good people. Arrogance breeds strife. If it comes easy it will

go easy. Heart ache after heart ache makes you sick. Ignore God's word and you will suffer. It's teaching is a fountain of life and makes for sound thinking and gracious living. A smart person applies knowledge. Irresponsible discussion make a real mess. Rebellion and homelessness go hand in hand. Souls who follow their hearts thrive. Become wise by walking with the wise. Disaster entraps sinners but people loyal to God get a good life that is passed down to their grandchildren. Banks foreclose on farms unless the poor lose their shirt to high priced attorneys. A refusal to correct is a refusal to love – love your children and discipline them. An appetite for good brings much satisfaction but the belly of the wicked always wants more.

Final Notes

God is offering a way to not only bless you, but your descendants. Because King David loved God, he was obedient, He offered his life in a fight that seemed hopeless against a giant. Not only did he survive but his family was blessed as well. God is asking us to trust him. To make the wisest investment we can by saving the lives of others through wisdom, careful words, humility and trust in God. By doing so, we are promised a seat at his dinner table... a table he refers to in Revelations, as a table of conquerors. We have abundant victory when we are willing to risk it all to follow God's plan. In doing so, we learn what God considers abundant living. Because of

Christ's obedience, we are saved.

A PRAYER TO MOVE YOUR MOUNTAIN

Most Gracious and Heavenly Father,

We walked into this lesson believing you were going to teach us the factors of financial freedom and intelligence, but instead you showed us what is most important to you. You desire us to be your disciples. Wiling to walk away from what looks right for what is right. Yes, you want to give us abundant life and help us to flourish, but we have to fully understand that this is the way to that place. Joy. Unspeakable joy will enwrap us when we find our children and our grandchildren trust you. Lord Give us this wisdom, to see the greatness and wonderful blessings that unfold as we mature and walk with you in excellence. Help us to seek wise counsel, place intelligent loving people before us. Grant us supernatural wisdom and discernment to walk through the right doors, to recognize fools that plan destruction and to avoid the pitfalls that so many of us quickly fall into. Lord, suture our lips when we should be quiet, be still and just wait for your deliverance. We love you and we thank you, we give you glory, honor and praise.

In Jesus Name, Amen.

Anointing

"NOW IT IS GOD WHO MAKES BOTH US AND YOU STAND FIRM
IN CHRIST. HE ANOINTED US, SET HIS SEAL OF OWNERSHIP
ON US, AND PUT HIS SPIRIT IN OUR HEARTS AS A DEPOSIT,
GUARANTEEING WHAT IS TO COME."
2 CORINTHIANS 1:21-22

In Context

Praise God! He understands that we struggle.
In fact, he has allowed us to struggle so that
when we get through the storm, we are able
to help our friends as they journey through the
storm. In the same way, God was there for us.
While we suffer, our suffering is not greater than
the blessing of Jesus. Our suffering for Jesus
is meant to make us stronger and to provide
healing. We are here (Paul and Timothy write this
letter to the church in Corinth), to help you go
forward in courage. We know you will make it. We
were in a horrible situation in Asia. We thought
we were going to die! Instead, it was the biggest
blessing. We were forced to trust God instead
of our own strength. God raises the dead, so our
situation was in good hands. He will continue to
save us time and time again too. Your prayers

and praise to God have helped tremendously. God ignited our faith in him, focusing only on him. He has allowed us to walk with pride, knowing and acknowledging it was all him. We are just keeping it real. We intended to visit you twice. But it didn't work out. We honor our word and do our best to keep it. Do we sound like liars... saying one thing then another, teeter tottering back and forth? God's YES is always yes. We try to embody that. God's yes within us is sure. It will not fail. Jesus is destined to complete it. The real reason we didn't come to visit you is because we did not want to inflict pain. We aren't watching over your shoulders to make sure you live righteously; your faith is yours.

Destined to Win

Whether I experience financial, physical, relational or spiritual unrest – God is my father. Recently, I was invited to speak at an event. The host asked me to speak, put my face and name on a flyer and was off to the races. I never thought to ask her about the topic, it was on the flyer I thought... entitled, "Purposeful Connections". So, I knew I could talk about that all day every day. Well, the day before, I find out what the real topic was: love relationships. She invited me based on the love "scenarios" in my autobiography, which included being molested at 8, being raped at the result of an internet date and a failed marriage (among many other poor choices). She even told me that she had another couple that met on the internet and did it the "right" way and was now married for 8 years. I was shocked and afraid. For context, the host and I had a falling out the year before after an event that I hosted, that she did not prepare for. She "winged it" and it was obvious to our guests. I realized at the last moment that she was setting me up for failure and that her attempt was to embarrass me. But, NO weapon formed against me shall prosper. I prayed to God. When I say, GOD was all up in that room... he was all up in that room. Initially, the woman got up to preach. I know God was using her... then she said, "I thank God that I was called to preach at a young age. That I knew my purpose. It protected me from doing things that would make my preaching to no effect. It kept me from making choices with my body that no one would want or expect me to preach after. I thank God for that." Then, there was a lot of talk about molestation by clinical panelists. Some of what they shared triggered deep emotions within me. I braced myself for a long day. Then, while there were four speakers, she made three of them keynotes while I and the internet couple joined them on a Q & A panel. A "roasting" of sorts, I imagine was her goal. I felt like that woman they brought to Jesus early in the morning to say look, we caught her in the act of sinning. But, again, I prayed. I prayed all day for me to decrease as God increased. At the end of the 5 and ½ hour conference, I was given the microphone. I shared my testimony in truth and with great power. How my journey did not depict my destiny. That the purpose God placed on my life when he breathed life into me would not fail... no matter how hard Satan tried to stop it. I talked about being molested and how it affected my behavior. How I made choices based on what people thought of me as opposed to what was right or wrong. How I became a gang member in high school. How I was violently raped. How I had to walk away from a 16-year marriage to follow Christ and save my family. Life will kick you in the stomach sometimes. But we overcome by our testimony. I am glad God didn't make me the holy and sanctified preacher on the lineup. He made me the living proof that his anointing doesn't fail. No matter how hard people try to kick you or put you down. You get back up and keep it pushing. God will never fail. He is faithful and our cups run over.

"THOU PREPAREST A TABLE BEFORE ME IN THE PRESENCE OF MINE ENEMIES: THOU ANOINTEST MY HEAD WITH OIL; MY CUP RUNNETH OVER." PSALM 23:5

In Context

God gives us everything we need. He allows us to rest in fertile places and journey in peace. He restores his children's souls to honor his name. Though we may see danger - he protects, corrects and directs us. He anoints us with his Spirit so much so, our cup runs over. He prepares a table for us in the presence of our enemies. Goodness and mercy follow us forever and I shall live in the house of The Lord forever.

Final Notes

God has been doing a new thing in me. He has changed the way I speak. No longer do I talk about what worries me. Instead, I speak and hear faith. I have learned that yes, hard times do come. They are hard to withstand or predict as they come and go as quickly as the wind. But my confidence is in God and the fact that he loves me has been proven time and time again. God has anointed me with his saving grace, his salvation. God promised to finish his work in me. So even when it is I that fail, God will as Paul writes, allow me to walk with my head held high. In my failing, I look to him. Even when Peter trusted, believed and walked on water, as his faith began to fail, he called on Jesus. We have been blessed with an abundant anointing... an oil that never fails. In fact, it is so abundant, that God has blessed us to encourage, strengthen and support our brothers and sisters in the faith when their spirits fall due to hardship. Be strong, have courage and trust God. He won't fail us.

A PRAYER TO MOVE YOUR MOUNTAIN

Most Gracious and Heavenly Father,

Thank you for the promise. Thank you for the abundant gift of anointing that cannot fail. You have blessed us immensely. Lord, we stand in prayer for our brothers and sisters in the faith. We ask that you strengthen us to be a blessing in their hard times. To be your hands and feet when they need us most. Lord, prepare our hearts to worship you. Endow us with an abundance of your Spirit, your grace and your love. We recognize that all things are not good, but they all work together for the good. Teach us, mold us, use us. Consecrate us for the Holy anointing that you have promised will never fail.

In Jesus Name, Amen.

Blessing

"EVERY GOOD AND PERFECT GIFT IS FROM ABOVE, COMING
DOWN FROM THE FATHER OF THE HEAVENLY LIGHTS, WHO
DOES NOT CHANGE LIKE SHIFTING SHADOWS."
JAMES 1:17

In Context

Count it all joy when trials come because they will
strengthen your faith making you perfect. Ask for
wisdom from our generous God believing in him
alone and he will give it freely without question.
Don't teeter totter between trusting God and
trusting the world because that will make you
unstable. We all fade like flowers, yet the poor
are honored and the rich are humbled. God does
not tempt us, but patience during testing and
endurance are awarded the crown of life. Desires
tempt us and cause us to fall, not God. All good
and perfect things come from God. He chose us,
birthed us in his word. How wonderful to know
we are his prize. We must be quick to listen,
slow to speak and slow to get angry. Our anger
is incapable of producing the righteousness of
God. Listen to God's word... get rid of the filth.
Obey it and know that if you refuse you are only

glancing at what life could be instead of living it full on. Control your tongue. Be true to who you say you are. True righteousness cares for the underserved: widows and children.

Blessed Beyond Words

Isn't amazing how much God can bless you... with just a whisper in your ear? For me, it was three words: I love you. We spend our entire lives searching for the kind of love God gives. We search high and low, praying to find the perfect mate that will blow our minds, penetrate our hearts and protect us from dangers seen and unseen. So, why don't we honor God like we should? Why don't we stop to appreciate the blessings instead of standing with our hands and lips stuck out? I think it's because sometimes God is so good, we take it for granted. Today, I want to choose God first. Above and beyond - as I heard a colleague say stop choosing the urgent over the most important. This has been where I have been and I believe God spoke to me when he had her say it. I have been blessed beyond words and I should behave that way.

"THE LORD IS MY SHEPHERD AND I SHALL NOT WANT."
PSALM 23:1

In Context

God gives us everything we need. He allows us to rest in fertile places and journey in peace. He restores his children's souls to honor his name. Though we may see danger - he protects, corrects and directs us. He anoints us with his Spirit so much so, our cup runs over. He prepares a table for us in the presence of our enemies. Goodness and mercy follow us forever and I shall live in the house of The Lord forever.

Final Notes
Blessings follow us every day. Whether we can see God working or not. He is. Our responsibility is to put him first. In prayer, in praise and in preparedness through the study of his word. Then, all these things will be added to us.

A PRAYER TO MOVE YOUR MOUNTAIN

Most Gracious and Heavenly Father,

Forgive us for not always putting you first. You have been so good and so wonderful. Help us to remember that you are our Father. That our trust should not rest in any other hand or bosom but yours. Help us to understand the power in obedience and that nothing we face is bigger than you. All these things we pray.

In Jesus Name, Amen.

Praise

"THROUGH HIM THEN, LET US CONTINUALLY OFFER UP A SACRIFICE OF PRAISE TO GOD, THAT IS, THE FRUIT OF LIPS THAT GIVE THANKS TO HIS NAME." HEBREWS 13:15

In Context

Always love your neighbor. Treat strangers with respect, you never know when you are entertaining an angel. Consider those imprisoned and those that suffer adversity as if it were you. In marriage, your bedroom is undefiled; outside of marriage you are judged by God. Be content, God is with you. In this, you will boldly say, "God is my help, I have no fear." Remember teachers of God's word, who live by faith, comparing life to action. Jesus will never change; he stays the same. Let your heart be led by grace, not strange worship that promises gifts. We are not permitted to indulge in the sacrifice that belongs to God. It is his and he deserves it, as Jesus as sacrifice gave his life to save us. We do not bear the gift of eternal life, but it is given through Christ Jesus. So, let us offer the sacrifice of continual praise to God. Share your love for God outside the church. Listen to godly leaders that are obedient to God and share his message with you. Help them don't hinder them. Pray for us that we do well and live honestly. May the Lord who lives, make you perfect in all you do in His name, which is well pleasing to Jesus. To Him be glory forever. Grace be with you all.

Blessed

The day God breathed life into me I was blessed. But I didn't realize it until the day he saved me from myself. Since that day, I have learned that God's love is the love that we desperately seek from others day in and day out. What we desire from people we get in abundance from God... if we choose to acknowledge it. The Lord has pushed me into a place of leadership from his vantage point by sending me on assignment. While leadership was never the area I wanted to be in, it is God's will and his delight that many of us on assignment bear the work with gladness. I remember God asking me to create my first commercial on air. It was during a time when I was facing homelessness. One of my largest clients walked away and I was desperately trying to survive. I just faced a Christmas without the ability to give my children gifts and our water had been shut off. My landlord in his kindness forgave our rent that month. God told me to create commercials that stated, "God is faithful." He had me create Facebook ads that said the same. In the commercial, I said, "I am blessed and I want to share my story with you." I was happy and excited to have a commercial but I thought it was strange for God to request. But, I was obedient. I did it. In this way, I was speaking blessings over my life exponentially. I heard Bill Winston say it like this, "Faith converts your humanity into divinity. Changing your vision, your speaking and your actions." That when we speak life into our lives, we believe the Word of God and we strengthen our faith. God responds to this. God had me create a commercial that gave him praise and pronounced a blessing over my life. How profound. Within 3 months of the commercial airing, God changed my client load. Not only had I replaced my top client, he sent an abundance of many more. I went from not having the money to do an annual Valentine's Day program with women to taking those women on a retreat in Dallas. I went from walking without a car for more than 6 months to purchasing a BMW X5. I went from struggling to get my bachelor's degree for over 10 years to getting a $7K scholarship to finish school within 3 months. I am in my promised land. I was blessed beyond words. Because I gave him praise in advance. Because I trusted him. Because I believed. I became the living proof that God is real, that prayer still works, that faith IS the substance of things hoped for and the evidence of things not seen. All I can do, is give him praise.

In Context

Lord, protect and defend me before my enemies. Confuse their way for they have devised evil against me. Let them be caught in their own net. In this my soul shall rejoice and be thankful to God. Everything in me shall say, who is like this God that saves the poor from his strong oppressor? Liars have risen their tongues against me. They have returned evil for good. Even though I served them with prayer and fasting in their time of need. I loved them like a brother. But when I fell, they rejoiced; joined together to persecute me. They mocked me during their feasts. How long Lord will you allow it? Rescue me. I promise to give you praise before the church and many men. Let not my enemies rejoice over my downfall, or wink their eyes at me though they hate me without cause. They don't speak peace but war against those that are silent in the land. Instead, they speak nonsense. Lord, speak: judge, defend, protect me. Let them not say they have the victory. Let them be brought to shame and confusion that rejoice at my hurt and magnify themselves against me. Let them shout for joy and be glad, that favor my righteous cause. Let the Lord be magnified which has pleasure in the prosperity of his servant. And my tongue shall praise thee all the day.

Final Notes

Our obedience shines a light on the love, mercy, grace and faithfulness of God. We are called to be blessed (not only in our personal, loving and intimate relationship with God as he reveals his love for us) before men as we walk and share the good news of Jesus Christ. God does not keep count as to whether we help one or many, but that we share him with a world that needs him. That doesn't mean that our enemies will give in. They may come even harder. This is when we lean and depend on our faith in God to see us through. We confess and believe that God will not allow us to be brought to shame. We praise him before many and before all to declare our trust, our faith and our dependence on God and God alone to see us through.

A PRAYER TO MOVE YOUR MOUNTAIN

Most Gracious and Heavenly Father,

We sing glory to your name. We are so very thankful that not only did you save us from ourselves and a world of sin, but you have blessed us with the gift of praise. A praise that should never leave our lips no matter our condition. Thank you for allowing us to see your power at work in us and around us. Help us to honor those that teach and live the Word of God before us. Allow us to be a help to our spiritual leaders and not a hindrance. Lord, protect us from our enemies. Give us supernatural insight to recognize our enemies for who and what they are. Rain excellent strategies, lifelong relationships, supernatural wisdom and abundant provision to help us fight on the battlefield with the courage, stamina, faith and trust in God alone to see us through. Let us stay strong and consistent, honoring you in all situations. Lord, strengthen our faith. Teach us, help us, direct us in your Word. Help us to confess your Word over our lives each day. Change us from being human to being divine, believing your Word will bring us into our faithful place and righteous end with you. That we may go forward and do the work that you have destined us to do. Forgive us of our sins. We give you all the glory, all the honor, all the praise.

In Jesus Name, Amen.

Gratitude

"AND BECAUSE OF HIS GLORY AND EXCELLENCE, HE HAS GIVEN US GREAT AND PRECIOUS PROMISES. THESE ARE THE PROMISES THAT ENABLE YOU TO SHARE HIS DIVINE NATURE AND ESCAPE THE WORLD'S CORRUPTION CAUSED BY HUMAN DESIRES."
2 PETER 1:4

In Context

Peter was a devout servant to Jesus. He desired to speak with those of faith. He starts by acknowledging that we have everything we need through Christ (full of glory and excellence). He also shares that Jesus has made many promises that empower believers to share in his divine nature and escape the corruption of this world that will entice worldly desires. For this reason, he asks that we conform our actions to Godly actions, with knowledge which leads to self-control, patience and endurance, and brotherly love for all. By doing so, we ensure a grand welcome into heaven when our work on earth is complete. He promises to keep reminding them of these things until his time on earth is over. This truth he shares is his affirming witness of Christ and why he is so confident to proclaim the message. The same message sent by God through the prophets. These words written will shine brightly like a morning star until the day Christ returns.

An Abundance of Gratitude & Strategic Prayer

Every year I host a program called, KYSE: Kiss Your Self-Esteem. For four years now we pamper and shower God's love on women the week before Valentine's Day to help them get unstuck and move forward into God's purpose and destiny. Similarly, I struggle financially to put it all together. It is a big investment. This year was no different. But, my strategy and application were different. I felt strongly in my spirit that God wanted me to call on his prayer warriors that I had a personal relationship with and ask them to pray. Some, I'd never prayed with before.... But they were in alignment with the Holy Spirit. It was so amazing. As we grew nearer, it didn't look like I was going to be able to make it happen. Clients refused to pay what they owed, others were indifferent and lied about attempting payment... but God made a way. I prayed each day for unwavering walk-on-water faith. I confessed the scriptures and thanked God in advance for what he would do. On the day of departure, I still didn't have everything I needed but I continued to move forward in faith. God worked it out! He in fact, showed up and showed out. We had such an amazing time. It was a memory the women will cherish for years to come and a time when God received all the glory! I am so thankful that I had faith in God and his promises! Jesus was a gift to me as I know it was his presence, his guidance, his angels encamped around us and the prayer warriors consistent, effective, fervent prayer that saw us through. At church on the last day of our retreat (Sunday), the minister preached, "Prayer Still Works!" How amazing is that? I was beyond grateful for the gift of strategic prayer and a God who answers all prayer.

"FOR GOD SO LOVED THE WORLD, THAT HE GAVE HIS ONLY BEGOTTEN SON, THAT WHOSOEVER BELIEVETH IN HIM WILL NOT PERISH BUT HAVE EVERLASTING LIFE." JOHN 3:16

In Context

Nichodemus, A prominent leader among the Jews approached Jesus late in the night. He told him, "We know that you are a man sent from God, otherwise you could not do all that you've done or teach what you've taught." "You are right," said Jesus. "Take it from me, only a person that is born again can see that I am pointing to God's kingdom." But Nichodemus was confused. "How can someone be born again if they've already been born and are grown up. No one can re-enter the womb. What do you mean when you say born again?" Jesus responded, "You are not listening. I'll say it again unless a person submits to this original creation-a baptism into new life, it's not possible to enter God's kingdom. When you look at a baby, it's something that you can see and touch. But the life inside the baby that is being formed, you cannot see or touch-that's because it is a living spirit." Jesus went on to share the comparison of the Holy Spirit to the wind and how one can't determine its origin or destination. But this confused Nichodemus even more. Jesus countered, "You're a respected teacher of Israel and you don't know these basic things. Listen carefully, I'm speaking the whole truth with you. I speak only what I know by experience. I give witness to only what I have seen with my own eyes-there's nothing second hand here, no hearsay. Yet, instead of facing the evidence and accepting it, you procrastinate with these questions. If I tell you things that are plain before your face and you don't believe me, what use is there in telling you things you can't see-the things of God. No one has ever gone up into the presence of God except the one who came down from that presence - the Son of Man. In the same way that Moses lifted the serpent in the desert so people could have something to say and then believe it is necessary for the Son of Man to be lifted up and everyone who sees him, trusting and expectant, will gain a real life-eternal life.

God loved us so much that he gave his son, his only son and he did it so that no one would be destroyed just by believing in him. Anyone can have a whole and lasting life. God didn't go to all the trouble of sending his son just to point an accusing finger, telling the world how bad it was. He actually came to help to put the world in a right space again. Anyone who trusts in him is acquitted and anyone who refuses to trust him has long since been under the death sentence without knowing it. Why? Because that person failed to believe in Jesus Christ when he was introduced to him. This is the mess that we are in: God sent his light into the world but men and women ran for the darkness. They went for the darkness because they weren't really interested in pleasing God. People that do evil are afraid that they'll be exposed if they come too close to the light. But anyone working and living in truth and reality welcomes the light, that the work of God can be seen." After speaking with Nichodemus, Jesus was relaxing on the Judean countryside with his disciples, he was also baptizing. John the Baptist had followers that saw Jesus as their competition. But John corrected them stating, "It's not possible for a person to succeed in the work of God without having help and you were there when I told the Pharisees that I'm not the Messiah, I am simply the one to get things ready. In fact, it's an honor for me to be at his side. I'm genuinely happy. The one who gets the bride is technically the bride groom and the bride groom's friend is the best man. How could I be jealous when I know that the wedding is finished and the marriage is off to a wonderful start? My cup is running over, it is his time to shine. God himself is the truth. God loves Jesus immensely. If you trust him, you receive his blessings - if you don't, you live in angry darkness.

Final Notes

An attitude of gratitude helps to appreciate every abundant gift Christ has provided. The Holy Spirit, the power of prayer, the gift of faith, mercy, unending love and the ability to share his love with others. It is amazing how faithful God is. If only we taste and see, we can reflect on every perfect gift God has provided and give him glory and praise for his exceedingly abundant plan for our lives.

A PRAYER TO MOVE YOUR MOUNTAIN

Most Gracious and Heavenly Father,

We thank you for the abundant gift of Christ which supplies everything we need. Help us to remember our walk is more important than our talk. Help us to see you in every situation and to take advantage of the opportunity to praise you. We love you and we bless your Holy and righteous name. Lord, we humbly ask that you impart supernatural wisdom and discernment that will lead to amazing strategies in business, financial awareness and genius to bless our families and your children, emotional well-being and healthy choices that will keep us strong and able to do the work you have purposed us to do. Thank you. Forgive us and help us to be all that you have created us to be.

In Jesus Name, Amen.

Jesus

"THEREFORE ALL THINGS WHATSOEVER YE WOULD THAT MEN SHOULD DO TO YOU, DO YE EVEN SO TO THEM: FOR THIS IS THE LAW AND THE PROPHETS." MATTHEW 7:12

In Context

Being critical of others will always be reflected to you. It's like a mirror. You can't wash your neighbor's face without seeing the dirt on your own. Honor God with holy regard. Don't make small of the Kingdom of God, it is to be held in High Regard. Ask God for what you desire. Be direct and don't play games. In the same way that you love your children, God loves you. Do for others what you would like them to do for you. Make God a priority. A good life with God requires your total attention... not shortcuts. Look out for thieves in the temple. They pretend to be holy, smiling in your face, telling you what you want to hear then they steal from you. We can tell if a man is real by his fruit. Just because a man claims to know God doesn't mean that God knows him. The foundation of truth is this: if you hear the Word of God and respond to it in obedience, you will be like a man that has built his house on a rock.

Life on the Rock

I have faced so many storms in my life. One thing I can confidently say is, "If it hadn't been for the Lord on my side, where would I be?" The day I confessed and BELIEVED in the name of Jesus, my whole world seemed to come together mentally. I began to understand that I am not always meant to know how things will end or why they happen. My soul responsibilities in this life are to trust, obey and love Jesus. When these three principles shape my life concerning the Lord it changes the way I walk, talk, perceive and do. It allows me to decrease my opinion or measurement of personal impact, influence and image. Which drives me to focus on increasing my ability to hear God, to do what he asks and to love others as he would have me to do. This isn't a perfect process and only happens when I wake up with an intention to serve God, to listen for his instruction and to sacrifice the urgent for the most important. Through prayer, studying and obedience (as God pushes me to do more and be more) I live a life of abundant blessings, love and immeasurable grace.

"JESUS REPLIED: 'LOVE THE LORD YOUR GOD WITH ALL YOUR HEART AND WITH ALL YOUR SOUL AND WITH ALL YOUR MIND.' THIS IS THE FIRST AND GREATEST COMMANDMENT. AND THE SECOND IS LIKE IT: 'LOVE YOUR NEIGHBOR AS YOURSELF.'

ALL THE LAW AND THE PROPHETS HANG ON THESE TWO COMMANDMENTS."" MATTHEW 22:37-40

In Context

Jesus compares the Kingdom of God to a lavish wedding banquet. One in which the master invites many that refuse to attend. Again, he sends for a set of invited guests. They all refuse and even beat up the servants that came to invite them. Finally, they invited any and all to join them. The banquet was full but the master noticed someone standing out. They weren't properly dressed and were immediately dismissed from the banquet. In this parable, Jesus teaches that many are called but few are chosen. At that moment, the Pharisees tried to test Jesus. Because of his impeccable reputation for integrity, they wanted to see if he believed in paying taxes, but Jesus understood. He said, "Render unto God what is Gods and unto Caesar what is his." Then a Sadducee, tried to trip him up regarding the resurrection, asking, "If a woman marries 7 brothers, in the resurrection who will she be married to?" Jesus responded that no man is dead in the resurrection, her intimacy is not with them but with God in heaven. Furthermore, God is not dead. He is the living God over living men (Abraham, Isaac and Jacob) as it is written in the Bible. The Pharisees return with one more question: "Which law is most important?" Jesus responded, "That you love God with all your heart, mind and soul.

And second is that you love your neighbor as yourself." After all of their testing, Jesus asked, "What do you think about the Christ? Whose son is he?" They responded, "David." Jesus then replied, "Well how do you explain that David calls the Christ his master in this scripture: "God said to my Master, 'Sit here at my right hand until I make your enemies your footstool." Now if David calls him 'Master', how can he at the same time be called his son?' The religious leaders ran away for fear of embarrassing themselves again.

Final Notes

God desires that we love him with all of our hearts and minds. He also desires that we honor and respect his image. This means that we are not just sweet talking ministers out there pushing the name Jesus on people like a sticker they give you when you vote. No, he wants us to be his hands and feet. Lovingly sharing his message and his love with the world, treating them the way we would want someone else to treat us. God is real. He is alive and he is paying attention. We have all been invited to his grandiose celebration of life in heaven, but we must learn, live and love the way he teaches us to treat his name, his kingdom and his people. In this is our greatest reward: an abundance of Jesus Christ who will be with us now and forevermore!

A PRAYER TO MOVE YOUR MOUNTAIN

Most Gracious and Heavenly Father,

How can we thank you enough for just being you! You are our everything. You are my thoughts. You are my love. You are my work. You are my every good intention. You are the me I become when I am trusting and believing and living for you. Thank you for faith to believe in greater! There is nothing we have, we can see, or imagine that does not have your intentional loving fingerprint all over it. Thank you Lord for blessing me and keeping me. Thank you for allowing me to be living proof that you save lives. Thank you for teaching me how to make better choices through adversity. Thank you for loving me in spite of me. Thank you for taking my sin and making it your own that I might spend today and eternity with you. The number of situations, intimate moments, revelations and faithful promises you have given don't compare to the infinite love you shower on me each day. I would be honored to spend eternity with you and I pray that I not only get to attend the wedding, but that I may be your bride.

In Jesus Name, Amen.

Impossible

"FOR WITH GOD NOTHING SHALL BE IMPOSSIBLE." LUKE 1:37

In Context

This chapter is the beginning of the story of the life of Jesus Christ... as studied and reported in the book of Luke. Zachariah and Elizabeth honored God yet were childless and older. An angel approached Zachariah and told him Elizabeth would become pregnant. The angel told him specific things the child could and could not do as he would be filled with the Holy Spirit and help people build a relationship with God. Zechariah doubted the angel and could not speak until the child was born. The same angel, Gabriel, later visited a virgin girl named Mary and told her that she too would become pregnant by the Holy Spirit. He foretold of the greatness her child would become and carry. He then told her that her cousin, Elizabeth was pregnant too... even in her old age. Then he said, "Nothing, you see, is impossible with God." Mary accepted the assignment and replied, "Let it be with me, exactly as you say." Mary immediately went to visit her cousin Elizabeth. There she stayed for three months and then returned home. Elizabeth went into labor and they named their son, John. Zechariah could also speak. He praised God for sending the Messiah, just as he'd promised.

Faithful

> Never has God let me down. If he brought me to it, he's always brought me through it. I remember planning an event for teens in Atlanta. I had no idea how I was going to pay for it, I just kept planning. I got speakers, volunteers, booked rooms, venues and more. It got down to the last couple of weeks and my prayers began to be answered. I couldn't have imagined how God was going to do it, but he did. I just operated in faith, trusting that he wanted me to do what he asked me to do and that he would provide.

"I can do all things through Christ, who strengthens me." Philippians 4:13

In Context

Stay on track, focused on God. God doesn't want his children holding grudges. Celebrate God all day, every day. Love on everyone in such a way they recognize, you are on their side. Rather than worry, pray. Praise God, thank him and then let him know what you need. Then you will have peace about your situation. Focus on whatever is true, noble, authentic, reputable, compelling and gracious. Love the best and disregard the worst. Then not only will it work out for good, but you will be a part of that. Love where you are – with much or little. We are content in the one who created us, we can survive any circumstance in him. God will take care of everything you need... his generosity exceeding yours in the glory that comes from Jesus. His glory is abundant through eternity.

Final Notes

We must recognize that all things are possible with God. He is abundant in all things. We don't have to worry or be concerned with tomorrow. We have every tool we need. The power of prayer, the power of his Word and the presence of his Holy Spirit. God is amazing and he is beyond faithful. All we have to do is believe.

A PRAYER TO MOVE YOUR MOUNTAIN

Most Gracious and Heavenly Father,

Thank you for the blessing and the power of your presence in our lives. It is an amazing feeling to know that we can depend solely on you... not in ourselves, our neighbors or even those in authority over us. You have all power. Help us to focus on what is good in our lives and to be content when we can't see what we desire. Help us to bring our concerns to you and leave them right there. Lord, you are so amazing and loving. We can't thank you enough. Lord as we chase whatever dreams you have placed in our hearts, direct us, shape us, teach us, protect us and surround us with your presence. Lord, open doors no man can shut and close doors no man can open. You are our rock, our shield and our exceeding great reward. Please, forgive us of our sins and thank you for abundant possibilities.

In Jesus Name, Amen.

Elegant

"HIS MOUTH IS MOST SWEET: YEA, HE IS ALTOGETHER LOVELY. THIS IS MY BELOVED, AND THIS IS MY FRIEND, O DAUGHTERS OF JERUSALEM." SONG OF SOLOMON 5:17

In Context

An exchange of two lovers unfold as they describe the emotional breadth of their love. The man describes her as his best friend and best lover, asking his friends to toast to life and love. As she responds that she was sound asleep with vivid dreams, asking the reader to listen to the knock of her lover. He begs her to let him in from the cold night. She explained that she was in bed and undressed, did he want her to get dirty? The more he knocked the stronger her desire became. She hurries to the door to find him gone. She goes out to search for him, but those that were supposed to guard the city beat her up and tore her clothes from her. Then asks her sister of Jerusalem to tell her lover if they see him that she is heartsick and she wants him back. They ask, "What makes him so great that you beg for our help?" She responds that his one of a kind, handsome (giving great detail) and his words were kisses and his kisses words. She added everything about him delights her through and through. That is her man.

Faithful

Have you ever been madly in love with someone? I have. My eldest daughter got married to her high school sweetheart yesterday. I can say she and her husband are madly in love with each other. They spend every moment they can with each other. I thought it was a little obsessive but they truly complete one another. I am not married today, nor am I in a relationship, but I remember those days! It is reflective of how I feel about the Lord... in a lot of ways. I want to wake up to his kisses (word), spend all day communing with him (prayer) and I truly run to the door each time he knocks (in Spirit). My day can't start or end without me acknowledging and spending time with him. I am head over heels in love with the God I serve, his name is Jesus. I would search the streets looking for him if I couldn't find him too!

"ABOVE ALL, LOVE EACH OTHER DEEPLY, BECAUSE LOVE COVERS OVER A MULTITUDE OF SINS." I PETER 4:8

In Context

Learn to think like Jesus. Consider your suffering a way to develop and train you to overcome sin. In this, you will be able to pursue God's will for your life. Don't worry about your old friends (the ones you used to sin with). You don't owe them an explanation. They will answer to God. Listen to the message from God provided by his prophets. They will live the life promised by Jesus. Be ready. Stay awake in prayer, love each other as if your life depended on it. Love covers a multitude of sin. Be generous with what God gave you. In this way, God will get the glory from your actions. When times get hard, know that Jesus suffered hard times too. God hasn't abandoned you. You are learning to persevere through tough times – it is a spiritual refining process. Count it all joy. If you did something wrong, that is different. But, if you are persecuted because of your Christianity, don't worry about it. As God's family, we are the first to be judged. If it is difficult for us, imagine what it will be like for those who do not believe. If you find life difficult because you're doing what God said, take it in stride. Trust him. He knows what he is doing and he will continue.

Final Notes
An elegant life of the believer is immersed in love! How wonderful and marvelous to be loved so greatly by the creator that if we miss his presence we earnestly chase after him? That we consider the love he gives so beautiful and marvelous, we cannot help but shower it on others. God is amazing. He is a perfect friend. Rather than allow us to go without suffering, he teaches us to persevere. He raises us as leaders (even conquerors) showing the way through our ability to withstand the persecution that comes

with following his instruction, while still being able to love and give him glory. This is the graceful life of the believer: abundant in elegance.

A PRAYER TO MOVE YOUR MOUNTAIN

Most Gracious and Heavenly Father,

I would have never considered my walk with you elegant! Filled with rugged adventure, unimaginable victories, excellent relationship and blessings beyond words... elegance is befitting. The grace that you have shown has been executed with machine-like precision: custom-fit and tailored just for me. How wonderful! Lord on this day, help me to love as you love me. Help me to give as you have given to me. Help me to forgive as you have forgiven me. Lord, bless me to not only become that elegant, life-giving conduit of your message and your love but align me strategically with your people. Help us create techniques, opportunities, educational institutions, businesses, organizations and tools that not only bless your people but reflect your love in a way that magnifies why we call you Father. Here we are Lord, send us. Send us to share your word, your love, your gifts and your message. We honor you. We uphold you. We love all that you are. Forgive us of our sins. We give you all the glory, honor and praise.

In Jesus Name, Amen.

Begin

"SO GOD CREATED MAN IN HIS OWN IMAGE, IN THE IMAGE OF GOD CREATED HE HIM; MALE AND FEMALE CREATED HE THEM."
GENESIS 1:27

In Context

In the beginning, God created the heaven and the earth... He said, "Let there be light" and there was light. God saw that it was good. Then he divided the light from the darkness. He called the light, "Day," and the darkness, "Night." The morning and the evening were the first day. God then created (by speaking and naming) the heaven, and divided the sea from earth. He created grass, trees, stars, sun and moon. He created every living thing on land and in the sea, birds in the air. He blessed them. He saw that it was good. Then God created man and woman in his image, in the image of God. He blessed them and instructed them to be fruitful and multiply. He gave them dominion over every living thing. He also assigned every herb, every fruit as meat. He also gave to every beast, bird and everything on the earth that has life, every green herb for meat. And he saw that it was good. He did all of this in 6 days.

A Fresh Start

I bought a brand new car not too long ago. I purchased insurance from a friend because I promised that I would. I try my best to keep my word. Well, I thought my insurance payments were a specific amount but found that I'd moved a dollar less into my personal account by accident. The payment was declined and the insurance company threatened to cancel my policy and also tacked on a $25 return check fee. It was understandable on the part of everyone involved. At some point I knew I placed too little over and transferred over that single dollar but I think I was just too late. At any rate, I really didn't want to pay that $25! LOL. I know it seems petty but I just didn't want to pay it when I simply forgot to move a dollar. But again, I was totally at fault. The lack of desire to go ahead and bite the bullet recalled a conversation I had with a friend who also used the same agent at one point. She remarked that the agents rates were really high and she saved a lot of money by switching to Geico. She sent me her agents name and number and I made the call. Guess what? I saved a lot of money by switching to Geico. It's hilarious because I work in marketing and yes, this is their brand promise! So, all day, I made a mention of this ironic notion that Geico lived up to their brand promise. In reflection, it means so much to me. It explains why Jesus was mad at the fig tree for advertising it was bearing fruit when it wasn't. I can only assume he cursed the tree because he was hungry and wanted fruit. I won't pretend I know that is why... but it would make sense. At any rate, how important is it that when we confess we want an abundant life that we take the actions that align with that? Consider how we call on the name Jesus. God has a brand promise to fulfill and so do we. Our new beginnings are birthed in our confession but realized when we commit to walk them out.

"BEHOLD, I WILL DO A NEW THING; NOW IT SHALL SPRING FORTH; SHALL YE NOT KNOW IT? I WILL EVEN MAKE A WAY IN THE WILDERNESS, AND RIVERS IN THE DESERT." ISAIAH 43:19

In Context

God said, "Don't be afraid. I redeemed you and I called you, you are mine." When you are in over your head or in rough waters, God will protect you. God is our Savior and he has paid a hefty price for us. That is how much he loves us and how much we mean to him. He is going to redeem us from every area: North, South, East, West. He is going to get everyone that bears his name back. He created us for His glory, personally formed each of us. There are many that cannot understand (see or hear) the Living God. But we know him, and trust him. We are his witnesses. He is the only God that is, was or will ever be. Once God creates, no one can uncreate it. God will fight our battles. He will turn the tables for us. But this powerful God asks that we be alert because he is about to do a new thing. He is creating a road in the desert. But as for the temple leaders, Israel and Jacob. They refused to pay attention, to give God his honor. Instead they continued to sin. Even though God forgave their sins, they refused to even give him sacrifices.

Final Notes

God creates by speaking it into existence. Then he gives it a name, a brand: Day.   In the same way, he created us. He created us to bring him glory. He also promises us that he will never leave us and that he will rescue us when we are in trouble. He promises to fight our battles. God called us into existence and created us for his glory. We are to honor our promises to him. Our words are containers of creativity and power. Our only responsibility is to know him, trust him and obey.

A PRAYER TO MOVE YOUR MOUNTAIN

Most Gracious and Heavenly Father,

Thank you for always being true to who you confess to be. As we live in a world full of people that pretend, we know you are God and you are God alone. Lord, thank you for calling us forth and naming us according to your perfect and precious brand. You are our rock, our shield and our exceeding great reward. Lord, as we continue on this journey, help us to stay focused, to be alert and aware and to witness as you do a new thing. God we declare and decree new beginnings, new opportunities, a new praise, a new worship and a fresh start. God in your abundant love and strategic plan you have set us forth on a path that only you could design. We thank you, we love you and we praise you.

In Jesus Name, Amen.

Forget

"BRETHREN, I COUNT NOT MYSELF TO HAVE APPREHENDED: BUT THIS ONE THING I DO, FORGETTING THOSE THINGS WHICH ARE BEHIND, AND REACHING FORTH UNTO THOSE THINGS WHICH ARE BEFORE, I PRESS TOWARD THE MARK FOR THE PRIZE OF THE HIGH CALLING OF GOD IN CHRIST JESUS."
PHILIPPIANS 3:13-14

In Context

Paul begins Chapter 3 with a warning to beware of evil workers and that we should never place our confidence in men. It is with the Spirit that we worship God. He remarks on his past as a professional and a devout Jew. In times past, he could easily remark on the power of his flesh. That is what he trusted and expected others to operate in, but now he forgets that part of his life. Instead, he is empowered by the Holy Spirit that is provided by Jesus to help him reach heaven... his goal. Paul shares that everything he gained with the flesh he counts as a loss in comparison to what he has gained in the Spirit with Christ. That his righteousness is not his own, but that through faith in Jesus his righteousness is from God. He notes that these things are possible through the price of death paid by Jesus and it is an honor to know him, to fellowship in his sufferings. This is his goal. It's not as if he has already arrived but that he is purposely driven forward with intention to meet the goal... leaving the rest behind that he may reach heaven. He shares that what is not right in us, God will reveal to us. He then asserts that others should follow him as he walks as an example. He also shares that many that began the walk are now enemies of the cross of Christ. Those enemies are driven by appetite and whose glory is in earthly things (which is their shame). Our conversation is in heaven, where we look for Jesus who will change our vile body that it may join his glorious body by his power.

It Is What It Is

Have you ever made a big mistake that you regret? Or maybe someone wronged you in such a way that you wish it never happened? One thing I have learned is that no matter how disturbing it is, we can't go back and change the past. When I was a young mother, I used drugs. This made me a horrible mother and very irresponsible. I lost a lot of friends, a lot of trust and ruined familial relationships. But, I can't change what happened. All I can do is move forward. Today, I speak to people who are or were where I was. I encourage them. I also speak to teens that may be facing a parent with a drug habit, or facing divorce and I encourage them. I was molested and raped as a young person. It shaped my perspective on life and sent me down a spiraling drain that almost took my life. But God. God saved me. Now he has helped me to better understand my purpose in life and that he NEVER makes mistakes. He designed me. He knew what I would face. He knew the decisions I would make. And while it was not ok, it is ok. Because Jesus makes all things new. While people may not throw our sins into a pool of forgetfulness, God does. We can walk confidently with Jesus knowing we are not perfect but that he is perfecting us. Once we learn to trust God's righteousness and his perfect plan, we are comfortable facing life everyday with an attitude of "It is what it is and I will do the best that I can do." The rest we leave to Jesus.

"COMMIT THY WAY UNTO THE LORD; TRUST ALSO IN HIM; AND HE SHALL BRING IT TO PASS." PSALM 37: 5

In Context

Don't worry about or desire to be like the braggers that think they are winning. In no time, they will wither like a cut flower in the sun. Instead, be open with and trust God. He will do what needs to be done and he will shine a bright light on you – vindicating you at high noon. Sit at his feet and rest. Pray. You don't have to fight your way to the top, they will fall in time being replaced by God's people. Don't argue, fight or get angry. God is laughing at them as they devise evil against his children. Less is more and more is less. A righteous man stands taller than many wicked, backed with God strength. Gods enemies will be stripped of their riches, while the poor righteous will have plenty. The wicked borrow and never return while the righteous give and give. Generous gets it all in the end. Young or old, I have never seen the righteous forsaken or their seed begging for bread. The righteous chew on wisdom like a bone and his heart pumps Gods Word like blood through veins. Wait on the Lord, you will get your seat in the sun. Stay focused on righteousness, it is from God and he will keep you safe. The Lord will help and deliver because you trust in him.

Final Notes

Forget what happened yesterday. Look forward and walk with Jesus. Don't get jealous of people who look like they are winning. In no time, God will vindicate you. In fact, you can sit at his feet and rest. Pray. God is laughing because he sees their end. Don't worry, you will get your moment in the sun. Let your past be replaced by abundant hope in a future that shines brightly in the presence of your enemies!

A PRAYER TO MOVE YOUR MOUNTAIN

Most Gracious and Heavenly Father,

Thank you for this word on today! Help us toss the ugly pain of yesterday into a sea of forgetfulness. Help us to forget those glory days when the ways of the world filled our hearts and minds but lacked a love for you. Lord, help us to remember that you are God and you are God all by yourself. While we are often surrounded by many enemies that wish to see us fall, you are in control. Lord, today you promised us that we stand tall amongst many enemies and that our pain will be replaced by laughter. Lord, help us to worship you in wholeness, in spirit and in truth. Help us to be everything you created us to be, rightly dividing the Word in truth. Help us Lord to be wise, with your will reflected in our actions, with your word in our hearts, with your spirit guiding us and with your love infused in everything we speak. Lord as we press forward to the high mark and calling, be with us. We can't make it to heaven without your grace, your mercy and your abundant love. Lord, direct us, protect us and correct us. Help us not to fall into the abundant desire this world presents on a platter each day but instead be filled with the wonder and amazement a generous heart can return when we are doing what you desire. Please forgive us of our sins. All these things we pray, giving you all the glory, the honor and the praise.

In Jesus Name, Amen.

Continue

"DEAR FRIENDS, LET US CONTINUE TO LOVE ONE ANOTHER, FOR LOVE COMES FROM GOD. ANYONE WHO LOVES IS A CHILD OF GOD AND KNOWS GOD." 1 JOHN 4:7

In Context

Everybody that says "God" is not true in faith. To test faith, listen for22 confession that Jesus is Lord, that he lived and died for our sins and that he is the Son of God. False teachers talk of God but refuse to acknowledge Jesus. We must continue to love one another because love comes from God. People who continue in love are born of God and have a relationship with God. Anyone who confesses that Jesus is God's son is in an intimate relationship with God. This is a love that comes from God. There is no room in love for fear. We will love and be loved, just as we were first loved by God. If anyone says they love God but continues to hate his brother or sister, they are a liar. You can't love a person you can't see if you cannot first love the person you can see. We must love God and people.

Abundant Strength to Love Again

When I worked for the television station. I began as a graphic designer creating on-air graphics, animations and running the graphics board for the newscasts. A sales rep loved my design work and attitude; went to the president and asked him to move me to sales... as her assistant. Many told me not to take the job. But, I felt like it was the right choice. The president told me I could make commission and they would teach me how to sell. (Honestly, this decision has blessed my company exponentially but that's a later story.) I did. At first, I failed. But, they didn't give up on me and before you know it, I was making an additional 1K to 1.5K a month in revenue. I loved my new position! Then, we got a new sales manager. He promoted me to Marketing Coordinator. (Yes!) But then, he took my commission. The difference left me in a deficit of about $400 – $500 a month. Wait. This was supposed to be a promotion but it felt like a demotion. He took my ability to sell away from siting a conflict of interest between marketing and sales. I was so angry at him, we argued everyday. He lost my trust. Eventually, he gained it back and even invited me to join Toastmasters. This allowed he and I to form a bond outside of work and allowed us to become friends. I could forgive him, and yes... joining Toastmasters has blessed my life as well. Just as he promised me it would. I am glad that

Jesus was guide and my friend... because I would have never forgiven him without staying in prayer and faith.

"THEREFORE, AS WE HAVE OPPORTUNITY, LET US DO GOOD TO ALL PEOPLE, ESPECIALLY TO THOSE WHO BELONG TO THE FAMILY OF BELIEVERS." GALATIANS 6:10

In Context

Forgive without judgment. Help the oppressed. Stay humble and focused on the assignment God has given you. Share with generosity what you have learned and your experiences. You cannot mock God. You reap what you sow. A person that ignores the needs of others is ignoring God. But, the person that plants in response to God harvests a crop of real and eternal life. We must continue to do good and not quit because during the right season we will harvest a good crop if we don't quit. Let us work to benefit all, starting with the people of faith. People that are "rule" keepers want one thing – to look good... rather than confess Christ's suffering and death. They don't even keep the law. They only want to boast that they have recruited you. It's more important to focus on what God is doing – not what we do. God is creating a free life for those that are his chosen people.

Final Notes

Pain is real. It can consume our thoughts, our best moments with family, our celebrations of victory... our everyday productivity. Pain is the reality that life won't always render the design we pictured in our minds. However, we do have the power to design how we react to specific situations. When we choose to love others despite the pain they have inflicted, to bless them when they need it most even when they continue to hurt us, to be stronger than what we see and feel... we continue in love. We prove that we are walking in a way that reflects a close relationship with a Savior that died for our sins. We exhibit an abundant strength to continue in love. We have to be generous and forgive. We must stay faithful and strong... continuing to do good to all. In due season, we will reap for our good works.

A PRAYER TO MOVE YOUR MOUNTAIN

Most Gracious and Heavenly Father,

Lord you are amazing. Your love is continuous. From the rising of the sun to the setting of the same, you don't change. You stay the same. Help us to be more like you. Help us to forgive those that despitefully use us. Help us to forgive those that have hurt us... whether intentional or accidental. Help us to keep walking in obedience trusting you, having faith in you and believing that we will see the goodness of the Lord in the land of the living. While we walk in faith, Lord see that we are camped in hope. Lord, direct our path and make it straight. Thank you for an abundant strength to continue in love. We know that you see us and that our living is not in vain. You are our rock, our shield and our greatest reward. Protect our families, friends and co-workers. Lord, lead our nation. Help us to be a good example of who you are and that you live in us. Forgive us of our sins and bless our today.

In Jesus Name, Amen.

Speak

"THE ONE WHO GUARDS HIS MOUTH PRESERVES HIS LIFE; THE
ONE WHO OPENS WIDE HIS LIPS COMES TO RUIN."
PROVERBS 13:3

In Context

Smart children take heed to parental instruction.
The good desire helpful conversation. Wisdom
and discretion in speaking preserves life. The lazy
want. The rich work for much but have nothing.
The righteous hate lies, loves to do right and has
a light that shines brightly. Only with pride comes
arguments. True wealth accrued by hard work.
Hope without completion makes a heart sick.
The law of the wise is a fountain of life. Good
understanding grants favor. Every prudent man
respects knowledge. Gossips fall into mischief.
Shame and poverty follows the one that refuses
to be taught. Hopes fulfilled please the soul. A
person that walks with the wise will be wise. Evil
chases sinners. A good man leaves his children's
children blessings. Investing in the poor reaps
wonderful crops. Punishment for your child is love,
sparing the rod is hatred. The righteous feeds

their soul.

Words of Wisdom

There is no doubt that words echo. They most impactful statements often play over and over and over again changing the way we see and think. For me, I remember when someone I loved and respected called me a slut. I remember when a friend told me to think about Future Stephanie today. I remember when a Pastor looked at me high on cocaine standing in his church and told me I was teaching Sunday School in two weeks. I remember when I told someone I loved them and they didn't respond. Words and even the absence of words echo. This is why it is vitally important that we wake with God on our mind and in our hearts. We need his words to echo in our minds each day: words of faith, words of wisdom, words of encouragement. Our faith grows when we hear the Word of God and when we listen to his prophets. The best question ever posed to me came from a drunk woman that witnessed me crying and afraid, she said, "Where is your faith?" It made me consider what she was talking about and a relationship with Jesus began. We must really watch what we say to ourselves, about ourselves and to our friends, family and co-workers. Our words have power and the power of life and death... rests in our mouths. Its not what we eat that makes us vile, it is what we allow to come out of us.

"WHO AMONG YOU IS WISE AND UNDERSTANDING?
LET HIM SHOW BY HIS GOOD BEHAVIOR HIS DEEDS IN THE
GENTLENESS OF WISDOM." JAMES 3:13

In Context

Be careful about teaching. Teachers are held to a very high standard and none of us are perfect. Controlling your mouth controls your life. Be careful of what you say; it has the power to create and the power to destroy. It only takes a spark to create a forest fire. Our words can ruin the world. We can tame tigers but we can't tame a tongue. Curses and blessings should not flow from the same mouth. Live well, live wisely, live humbly – this is wisdom. A holy life is categorized by getting along with others. It is gentle and reasonable, overflowing with mercy and blessings. Hard work and intentional positivity in relationships results with a robust and healthy community of righteous friendships.

Final Notes

Our words are wonderful because they carry an immense power to set things in motion. They can create beauty or they can destroy souls. We must exercise wisdom when speaking because it can not only harm ourselves, but it can really destroy others too. We must be respectful and intentionally try our best to get along. This is possible if we work hard and focus before we speak.

A PRAYER TO MOVE YOUR MOUNTAIN

Most Gracious and Heavenly Father,

Thank you. Your words give us life. You are the living Word. Help us to choose wisdom and to truly think before we speak. Help us to choose life. Help us to be positive in tough situations. Help us to be respectful, when we are being disrespected. Help us to remain humble, when we want a little glory. Lord, help us to keep our hearts pure – listening, absorbing, meditating – that we might live according to your Word. Help us to commune with the Holy Spirit and allow him to intercede on our behalf. Help us to recognize the power of words and help us to suture our lips when we should be quiet, be still and just listen.

In Jesus Name, Amen.

A Table in the Presence of Your Enemies

"THOU PREPAREST A TABLE BEFORE ME IN THE PRESENCE OF MINE ENEMIES: THOU ANOINTEST MY HEAD WITH OIL; MY CUP RUNNETH OVER." PSALM 23:5

In Context

God gives us everything we need. He allows us to rest in fertile places and journey in peace. He restores his children's souls to honor his name. Though we may see danger - he protects, corrects and directs us. He anoints us with his Spirit so much so, our cup runs over. He prepares a table for us in the presence of our enemies. Goodness and mercy follow us forever and we shall live in the house of The Lord forever.

They Tried to Destroy Us

"She is not God," an elderly phone bank volunteer for the campaign proclaimed. After making several calls for our candidate we'd discovered some dirty shenanigans by our opponent. Everything from calling the local newspaper to spread gossip to telling constituents at the door lies... it was getting ugly. They were pulling up our yard signs and throwing them in the streets, posting ugly things on Facebook and everyday it continued, I saw my candidate get weaker and weaker. In our lowest moments, we leaned and relied on our faith in God to see us through. We turned off what we heard, what we saw and only listened with our hearts. We KNEW God was on our side. We played fair. We didn't play politics. Then... it happened. An ad with more than 30 local pastors was released in two prominent newspapers... and they were endorsing our opponent. We'd heard the rumors but two days before the election, it was true. Our hearts dropped and the numbers did too. Fear tried to come in but we prayed and prayed and worked hard. We didn't stop until the polls closed... then we went to ever poll in our precincts trying to calculate the outcome. As our phones blew up with text after text we refused to look at them until we could determine the outcome. Finally, at our last two polls, we knew – WE WON!!! It was an amazing moment that no one could take from us. After all the dirty tactics, there was none left to throw. God vindicated us in an amazing victory!

"LOOK! I STAND AT THE DOOR AND KNOCK. IF YOU HEAR MY VOICE AND OPEN THE DOOR, I WILL COME IN, AND WE WILL SHARE A MEAL TOGETHER AS FRIENDS. THOSE WHO ARE VICTORIOUS WILL SIT WITH ME ON MY THRONE, JUST AS I WAS VICTORIOUS AND SAT WITH MY FATHER ON HIS THRONE."
REVELATIONS 3:20-21

In Context

In Revelations 3, a letter is written to each of the churches in Sardis, Philadelphia and Laodicea. To Sardis, God warns: I see you working but not for me. I know that you are busy but you are focused in the wrong direction. Return to what you heard originally and work in your purpose. To Philadelphia, He assures: I have seen you working hard to keep my word. Even when it was hard for you, you still believed. There are many that call themselves righteous but aren't being real. Hold on to your crown tightly and don't allow distractions to pull you away. When all is said and done, I will exalt you before them and all will know who really worshipped me in wholeness and truth. To Laodicea, God warns: Get it together. You teeter totter between good and evil but it would be much better if you make a choice to be one or the other. I am here because I love you and I want the best for you. Listen, I am standing at the door knocking. If you let me in, I will come in and eat with you. At my table, I sit among conquerors... Because only conquerors sit at the table in a place of honor. Just as I have conquered and sit at the side of my Father.

Final Notes

Isn't amazing that living for God results in a life of safety with him. Will we experience hardship and unfair situations? Yes, but our job is to remain faithful and trust God to vindicate us. It is not our job to get even or "make it right." Instead, we can walk in faith, knowing that God IS on our side! We can make any choice but we know the right choice. Wisdom is the application of knowledge. Let's put what we know to work.

A PRAYER TO MOVE YOUR MOUNTAIN

Most Gracious and Heavenly Father,

You are so awesome and amazing.
I know that there are many suffering today and life just really seems unfair. It is painful and not cool on so many levels. But Lord, you promised that you would see us through and that no situation or experience has power over you. You have the key to every door and make every situation work out for the good. Lord, we confess that we trust you. That we believe you, that we honor you. Help us to be everything you created us to be and thank you for your unending love, mercy and grace. Help us to be your hands and feet and willing workman focused on the purpose you have placed before us. Help us to be perfect conduits of your message and love.

In Jesus Name, Amen.

Next

"AND THIS I PRAY, THAT YOUR LOVE MAY ABOUND STILL MORE
AND MORE IN REAL KNOWLEDGE AND ALL DISCERNMENT."
PHILIPPIANS 1:9

In Context

Paul & Timothy write a letter to the church in
Philippi. They write: I thank God for you and
pray for you. For your association in the gospel,
knowing that he that started a work in you will
finish it until Jesus returns. Even as I consider
this, I acknowledge you are my partners in grace.
I pray that your love grows and grows as you
gain knowledge in judgment. That you approve
things that are excellent and sincere without
offense until Christ returns. My life in prison has
been given as an example to encourage others
to speak the gospel without fear. Whether
they preach as an opportunity for fame in
my absence or preach with sincerity and of
love – the word is preached. I celebrate that
Christ is preached; that everything he wants
accomplished to me and through me is done. I
long for the day to spend eternity with Christ but

I know I have a lot of work here to do. One day we will meet again, until then – live a life that honors Christ. Don't base your actions on my attendance or ability to judge them. Stand united, singular in vision, helping people trust God. Your courage and unity will reflect what they are up against – victory for us, defeat for them because you trust in God. The struggle is part of the journey.

Knowledge, Wisdom and Discernment

One of my co-workers wanted to note the time on her time card to reflect that we came back from lunch on time. But, we were late. I didn't want to do it. I refused. She smiled as though she were smarter than me and we went on about our business. Later that evening, the manager came to question me about a customer complaint. The incident occurred while we were away at lunch. If we were in office as we were supposed to be, we would have been able to take care of the client. Because her time card reflected she was there, he went to her next. She had to lie to cover up her lie and this time she lied on the client as well. I did not say a word, but the manager knew she was lying. Because the manager was there. And they tried to find us but we were out to lunch. She got fired that day for being dishonest, I was spared because I was honest about taking a lunch that was longer than expected.

"A WISE MAN WILL HEAR AND INCREASE IN LEARNING. AND A MAN OF UNDERSTANDING WILL ACQUIRE WISE COUNSEL."
PROVERBS 1:5

In Context

Proverbs was written to share wisdom for the young and old: Start with God, honor him and respect him. Listen and apply what your parents teach you. Bad friends will destroy you... no one robs a bank while everyone is looking but that is what they do. When you grab all you can get, the less you are. Wisdom shouts and begs you to pay attention. But instead you wait until it is too late when wisdom cannot help. Instead, wisdom replies, "Because you hated knowledge and refused to fear God, refused my advice and brushed every opportunity to help you away, you have made your bed. Lie in it. How do you like it?" Carelessness kills, complacency is murder. Pay attention to wisdom, then relax. Now you are safe.

Final Notes

Wisdom has a perfect work. We can abundantly chase what is next in our lives when we make Jesus our best friend and wisdom our sister. In God, we can trust that he will finish the work he started in us. We can do this with a knowledge that he chose us, we did not choose him. We may not be perfect but he is. His grace is sufficient because in our weakness is his strength made perfect. So, while we choose to exercise wisdom, it is to no affect without the accompaniment of Christ. We must acknowledge, love and respect God first and exercise wisdom second. In this way we can abundantly chase our "Next" in life.

A PRAYER TO MOVE YOUR MOUNTAIN

Thank you for this lesson. I think we often have to be reminded of our priorities in Jesus before we can really expect to grow, be more or obtain more. Lord help us to decrease as you increase. Grant us supernatural wisdom and discernment to make choices that are pleasing in your sight. Help us to expect your favor, your grace, your mercy, your goodness, your presence and your love. Help us to speak the word over our lives and by doing so, strengthen our faith, diminish our unbelief and move the mountains of fear that try their best to question our faith. We love you. We praise you. We need you. We abundantly chase what is next! In Jesus Name, Amen.

Abundance

"THE THIEF COMETH NOT, BUT FOR TO STEAL, AND TO KILL, AND TO DESTROY: I AM COME THAT THEY MIGHT HAVE LIFE, AND THAT THEY MIGHT HAVE IT MORE ABUNDANTLY." JOHN 10:10

In Context

A good shepherd will enter by the door (not climb over or sneak in the gate). He will call to his sheep, they will recognize his voice, and he will lead them out. They won't follow a stranger... they will run from him. This was a parable Jesus used to explain his role in the life of a believer. He explains that he provides the entrance to everlasting life. That the religious leaders before him were thieves. If you enter in with Jesus, you shall be saved, walk in purpose and find pasture. But the thief comes to kill, steal and destroy but he has come to give life – abundant life. The good shepherd gives his life for the sheep. The hired man runs because he doesn't care about the sheep. But Jesus knows his sheep. And other sheep – not of this fold, will hear his voice and all will become one-fold, with one shepherd. I give my life away and have the power to come back to life. This made people think that Jesus was evil, but others defended him based on his miraculous powers. Then they pushed him to reveal his true nature. But Jesus told them, he already has but they chose not to believe. Then he reiterates, "my sheep hear my voice, they shall never perish neither shall any man pluck them out of my Father's hand." Then the Jews tried to stone him because they considered him a blasphemer. Jesus provided scripture that rationalized his thinking then said, "If I do not the works of my Father, believe me not. But if I do, if you do not believe me, believe the works: that you may know and believe, that the Father is in me and I in him." They tried to kill him again, but he escaped to the place where John first baptized. The people flocked to him and said, "John did not perform miracles but everything he told us of this man is true." Many believed him there.

Saved, On Purpose and Found Pastures

Before I was "really" saved, I was a drug addict (among many other things). After I got saved, not only was I able to turn away from drug use, but I was also given purpose and a reason to walk with intention. For me, it was to help any person transition to their next level. This manifested itself in many ways: programs for women that were stuck, devotionals like this one, teen etiquette classes and finally in business. A true revelation of God's love for me helped me to love myself.

Which led to positivity, peace and purpose.

"HONOR THE LORD WITH YOUR WEALTH AND WITH THE FIRSTFRUITS OF ALL YOUR PRODUCE; THEN YOUR BARNS WILL BE FILLED WITH PLENTY, AND YOUR VATS WILL BE BURSTING WITH WINE." PROVERBS 3:10

In Context

Keep the commandments, they will provide long life and peace. Keep mercy and truth in your heart... with that you will find favor and good understanding in the sight of God and man. Trust in the Lord and lean not to your own understanding, in all your ways acknowledge him and he will direct you. Depart from evil and don't be wise in your own eyes, it will be healthy for you. Honor the Lord with the first fruit of your increase and your barns will be filled with plenty and thy presses shall burst with new wine. Don't despise God's correction, who he loves he corrects, even as a father the son in whom he delights. Happy is the man that finds wisdom it brings long life, riches, pleasantness and peace. Wisdom makes everyone happy that utilizes her. Do not be afraid, the Lord will be your confidence. Withhold not good to whom it is due, when you have the power to do it. Don't say to your neighbor go and come back later, when you can do it now. Devise not evil against your brother seeing that he is secure in your presence. Envy not the oppressor and choose none of his ways. The curse of the Lord is in the house of the wicked. Surely, he scorns the scorners but grace is given to the lowly. The wise shall inherit glory, but shame will be the promotion of fools.

Final Notes

So when people hear the word abundance they think, "baller alert" or like they used to say on the Beverly Hillbillies "big screens, movie stars, fancy cars and swimming pools". We all want that type of abundance in some way or another. But God is offering us a greater gift – unconditional love, peace and security. Jesus is our Boaz (ladies). But even beyond that, he promises us financial blessings as well. It comes from being obedient. Everything abundant comes from trusting God, exercising wisdom, walking in obedience and moving forward in faith.

A PRAYER TO MOVE YOUR MOUNTAIN

Most Gracious and Heavenly Father,

Thank you for being our shepherd. So many situations arise in our lives where uncertainty tries to rule the day, but Lord in those moments we ask for clear direction. Lord, please rain your wisdom on us. Help us to drown out the distractions and hear your voice with clarity and certainty. Lord, grant us the wisdom to make the changes in our life that will bring peace, positivity and purpose. Help us to prosper in spiritual acuteness, emotional wellness, healthy choices, strategic mental growth and financial blessings. Lord, we know that we are not perfect. Help us not to be wise in our own eyes and forgive us of our sins. We confess that you are Lord, that you died for us, that you rose and live today. We confess that you are God and you are God alone. Direct our paths and make them straight. Help us to be a blessing to someone else today.

In Jesus Name, Amen.

Grace

"SHE WAS TAKEN TO KING XERXES IN THE ROYAL RESIDENCE IN THE TENTH MONTH, THE MONTH OF TEBETH, IN THE SEVENTH YEAR OF HIS REIGN. NOW THE KING WAS ATTRACTED TO ESTHER MORE THAN TO ANY OF THE OTHER WOMEN, AND SHE WON HIS FAVOR AND APPROVAL MORE THAN ANY OF THE OTHER VIRGINS. SO HE SET A ROYAL CROWN ON HER HEAD AND MADE HER QUEEN INSTEAD OF VASHTI." ESTHER 2:16-17

In Context

King Xerxes asked his queen to dance for his friends during a celebration, she refused and embarrassed him. He decided to find a new queen. Just as he was about to change his mind, his servants suggested he begin to search for a new queen. After finding several suitable virgins, his eunuch would put them through various beauty treatments. He liked the idea and approved it. Mordecai, a Jew, raised his cousin Hedassah (Esther). The was gorgeous. Esther was brought to the kingdom as a potential queen. The eunuch liked Esther. He ordered special food for her, assigned seven personal maids and gave her the best rooms in the harem. Mordecai warned Esther not to tell anyone about her heritage and she didn't. After a year of beauty treatments, each virgin was allowed to meet with the king. Each virgin, after her visit was allowed to take a special gift of her liking. When Esther met with the king, she only took what her eunuch advised. Everyone loved Esther. The king fell in love with Esther far more than any of his other women or the other virgins. He placed a royal crown on her head and pronounced her queen. At a celebration, her cousin Mordecai was sitting at the King's Gate. Two of the kings's eunuch's (the ones who guarded his entrance), planned to kill him. Mordecai learned of the plot, told Queen Esther who told King Xerxes, giving credit to Mordecai. After confirmation, the men were killed.

Grace and Favor are Jewels in the Crown of God

I have never in my life felt so fulfilled as I have as a child of the Most High God. I never really loved myself or found myself important enough to be considered anyone or anything. It wasn't until I actually began to hear the voice of God through his word that my purpose for life became clear. All roads lead back to Jesus. It doesn't matter what you were created for, if you are doing it right, one day, the person you serve will thank God that you were where you were doing what you were doing to help them along the way. For me, that person is my pastor in Atlanta. His name is Pastor Charles Odom. Pastor Odom saw past my drug use. He saw me. His vision of me allowed me to see a small glimpse of me. His investment and belief in me meant and still means the world to me. All he asked me to do was teach Sunday School. But, it meant that he still saw hope when I couldn't see it in myself. I am so grateful for the grace and mercy God has extended but in that moment, I felt God's divine favor that said, "Stephanie, keep going, don't give up. I am right here and I am not letting you go."

"BUT HE GIVES US MORE GRACE. THAT IS WHY SCRIPTURE SAYS: "GOD OPPOSES THE PROUD BUT SHOWS FAVOR TO THE HUMBLE." JAMES 4:6

In Context
Fighting, arguments and war come from selfish desire. We are willing to steal, kill and destroy for what we want rather than ask God for it. This is because most the time we want to consume what we don't need in lust. God cares, in fact he's jealous. He gives love far better than anything you are trying to obtain. It's common knowledge that God opposes the proud, but he shows favor to the humble. So let God work his will in you. A quiet yes to God will invite his presence. The devil will flee if you resist him. Purify your inner life and stay far away from secret sin. Face your moment of truth... and get serious. Don't meddle or talk about each other. Let God be God. You can't determine tomorrow. Instead, say, "If it is God's will, we will do this or that." As it stands we are

too proud. An oversized ego is evil. If you know the right thing to do and choose not to do it, that is evil.

Final Notes

Abundant grace and favor are ours. God has crowned us with a beautiful gift if we simply accept it without chasing what the world calls, "good". God's love is so amazing and powerful. But, while we are blessed with abundant grace and favor, we are still expected to walk in humility and with wisdom.

A PRAYER TO MOVE YOUR MOUNTAIN

Most Gracious and Heavenly Father,

You are so beautiful: full of mercy and grace. Lord, we thank you for your love. On this day, help us to exercise true wisdom. Help us to be stronger than we think, smarter than we know, humble and willing to live a life that honors you before men. Lord, thank you for placing your super on our natural. We are absolutely nothing without you. Help us to desire to do your purpose and will above our own selfish desires. Lord help us to love others without condition.

In Jesus Name, Amen.

Sacrifice

"THE SACRIFICES OF GOD ARE A BROKEN SPIRIT: A BROKEN AND A CONTRITE HEART, O GOD, THOU WILT NOT DESPISE."
PHILIPPIANS 1:9

In Context

David pleas for forgiveness and mercy, admitting his sins before God. He asks God to renew him and begs him not to toss him aside. He promises to teach others that are lost how to find God. He promises to praise God. He knows that pretending doesn't work and that true worship pleases God. This was a lesson he learned when his pride was stripped. He recognizes that all men will bow when their world is torn apart. Delight in us, rebuild us, he prays, that we may worship you with true righteousness.

Admitting When We are Wrong: The Moment of Truth

A dead baby, a broken marriage and an unforgiving spirit tormented me day in and day out for up to 2 years. When you wake up and see that person in the mirror, you can't help but cry. I remember the day my husband and I went to have the abortion. He could see it was eating me alive and offered me a way of escape. But, I forced myself forward and probably destroyed the life of the only son I may have had. It took a long time for me to forgive myself. I was empty, depressed and like David, begging for a reprise. Instead, I pummeled deeper and the situations, choices and decisions that transpired after were horrific. Today, praise is not a sacrifice. God saved me from myself. I made a lot of wrong decisions and I still do. But, I am grateful I know a Savior that loves me enough to pick me up when I fall and helps me to stand on solid ground again.

"THROUGH JESUS, THEREFORE, LET US CONTINUALLY OFFER TO GOD A SACRIFICE OF PRAISE—THE FRUIT OF LIPS THAT OPENLY PROFESS HIS NAME." HEBREWS 13:15

In Context
Be at peace and good to others, loving and supplying need when you can. You never know when you might be entertaining angels. Love the prisoners, the abused and the married with respect, treating each as if you were in their situation. God does not favor casual and illicit sex. Don't chase material things. God will supply all of your needs. Appreciate your pastors, watch how they live it should line up with what they speak. Jesus doesn't change. Products named after Christ don't seem to do much, don't buy the hype. Jesus died for us outside of the city gates.

His blood was brought within and used to cleanse our sins. So, we too must leave the safety of the city to help save those that are still outside the gates. Let us praise Jesus in the streets. Don't take your situation for granted and fail to do the work. God takes pleasure in worship and different sacrifices made to serve his people. Be responsive to pastoral leaders and contribute to their work with joy. Pray for us. May God make Prophecyyou perfect in every good work to do his will. Working in you through Jesus what is perfect in his sight. To him be glory forever and ever.

Final Notes
Abundance requires that we admit when we make a mistake and pray for forgiveness. It also requires that we give God glory and praise. It requires that we respect and seek to help others, including our pastoral leaders with joy and love. Abundant sacrifice pleases God. It lets him know that you are willing to walk in your moment of truth and thank him for always being there no matter what state you are in. This is the true gift of Abundance – it makes all things new and beautiful.

A PRAYER TO MOVE YOUR MOUNTAIN

Most Gracious and Heavenly Father,

You are our rock, our shield and our exceeding great reward. Your grace is sufficient, for in our weakness is your strength made perfect. You bless us in spite of us and we can't help but give you glory, honor and praise. Lord, on this day we pray for a unique communion with your Holy Spirit. Speak to us in profound ways, revealing where we may have fallen and revealing where we have served you well. Direct our paths and make them straight. Help us to be at peace with all, despite their choices and behavior. Help us to love and respect others, no matter their condition or our preconceived thoughts concerning their position. You are our rock. We stand and lean and depend on you. We need you right now to guide us and make us sure that the way we live our lives will reflect the abundant lives you desire to give us. Help us to live lives that are full of love, of investing in others, of forgiveness – even if that means forgiving ourselves, mercy toward others and respect to those that are suffering with low self-esteem or the harshest of life circumstances. Help us to be a perfect conduit of your love, your message, your mercy and your grace.

In Jesus Name, Amen.

Joy

"WHEREIN YE GREATLY REJOICE, THOUGH NOW FOR A SEASON, IF NEED BE, YE ARE IN HEAVINESS THROUGH MANIFOLD TEMPTATIONS: THAT THE TRIAL OF YOUR FAITH, BEING MUCH MORE PRECIOUS THAN OF GOLD THAT PERISHETH, THOUGH IT BE TRIED WITH FIRE, MIGHT BE FOUND UNTO PRAISE AND HONOUR AND GLORY AT THE APPEARING OF JESUS CHRIST: WHOM HAVING NOT SEEN, YE LOVE; IN WHOM, THOUGH NOW YE SEE HIM NOT, YET BELIEVING, YE REJOICE WITH JOY UNSPEAKABLE AND FULL OF GLORY: RECEIVING THE END OF YOUR FAITH, EVEN THE SALVATION OF YOUR SOULS."
I PETER 1:6-9

In Context

Peter shares the joy that comes from faith in Jesus Christ with the people scattered in Pontus, Galatia, Cappadocia, Asia and Bithynia. To those that know God in the Spirit, whose righteousness is from Jesus Christ, grace and peace. Blessed is God who has provided through Jesus a perfect inheritance, kept by the power of God through faith. For this reason, we rejoice, even if in this moment it is difficult, our faith through testing will be more precious than gold. We will continue to praise, honor and give glory until Christ returns. Even though you haven't seen him, you love him through faith which gives unspeakable joy. This will lead to salvation. Prophets have searched and testified about this. You know this by power of the Holy Ghost; this is what angels desire to consider. We are to be holy, as Christ has called us to be. Your journey requires that you walk with God in reverence; he will help you when you call. There was a heavy price paid for our salvation. Follow the truth, love others, become new again through God's living word which lives forever.

A New Life

When I moved back to Oklahoma from Virginia, there was a new life waiting for me. But, I thought I was returning to my old life. A life that was filled with pain, low self-esteem and poor choices. But, God had a different plan. He wanted me to return home and show the people that knew me before that I was different... that I changed in Jesus name. He gave me a new life, full of adventure and promise. I definitely experienced hard times but this was certainly not that. No longer a drug addict, no longer married to a man that didn't appreciate me, no longer pitiful me. Instead, I returned with a faith in a power that was much bigger than me and completely capable of fighting every battle. I began to plant seeds of greatness in others with seemingly no financial backing to support the dream. But every endeavor was met with provision. I was living proof that faith in God loves, heals, restores, promotes and completes you. Every battle is his and not mine.

"UNTIL NOW YOU HAVE NOT ASKED FOR ANYTHING IN MY NAME. ASK AND YOU WILL RECEIVE, AND YOUR JOY WILL BE COMPLETE." JOHN 16:24

In Context

Jesus shares with his disciples: Prepare to be ostracized for my sake. They will think they are doing the work of God. Even though I have told you I will leave, you don't ask where I am going. Instead, you have become sad. He goes on to share that by leaving he will send a comforter and friend in the Holy Spirit. The Holy Spirit will guide you into all truth and honor Jesus. He added, "In a day or so you're not going to see me, but then another day you will see me." This made them question the meaning of what Jesus shared. He told them to you will be sad but the world will throw a party. But your sadness will become joy. Much like a woman about to give birth to a baby. She is in great pain during labor but once the baby is born there is great joy. This will be similar for you. Ask the Father for whatever is in his will. Ask in my name, according to my will, and he'll most certainly provide that you may obtain joy. I came from the Father and return to the Father. The disciples responded that now they understood that Jesus did come from God. Jesus asked, "Do you now believe?" There will come a day when you will be scattered and leave me alone. I am not alone because the Father is with me. These things I have I spoken to you that you might have peace. The world will give you trouble, but be of good cheer, I have overcome the world.

Final Notes

Abundant joy requires that we leave the pain and troubles of this world to God. That we walk by faith knowing that God has it all under control. We will have hard times, this is inevitable. But, we will also have good times. Our joy does not come from what happens to us in this world, it comes from the relationship we have with Jesus. In this relationship, there is joy everlasting that leads to salvation. There is a scripture that says, "Better is one day in your courts than a thousand anywhere else." This is so true when you realize how strategic, loving and on purpose God is concerning our lives. What we see, feel and react to today is no surprise to God! Let us stand strong, hold our heads high, thrust tightly to our chests the confession of true joy and faith with a heart that can't be moved by situation.

A PRAYER TO MOVE YOUR MOUNTAIN

Most Gracious and Heavenly Father,

Lord we come to you shouting victory and embracing joy. We love you and choose life. We speak life. We speak truth. We speak abundance! Lord, you promised us that if we simply ask, according to your will, that our prayers would be answered that our joy may be full. You said unless the Lord build the house, we labor in vain. You promised us that if we commit our works to you, our plans would be established. Lord on this day we confess, every job, every business, every child, every thought we want you to engineer, to take hold of and consider. Lord, decrease us and increase you. Forgive us and help us to be all that you created us to be. Lord, we have joy and it is a joy that the world didn't give so it certainly can't take it away.

In Jesus Name, Amen.

Eternal

"TRUST IN THE LORD FOREVER, FOR IN GOD THE LORD, WE HAVE
AN EVERLASTING ROCK." ISAIAH 26:4

In Context

Isaiah shares that right living people have
a strong city in salvation. These people are
dedicated to and depend on God. They do not
quit. The path of right living people is level. They
do not rush but are patient, and happy with the
journey God has prepared. They are content
with who God is and what he has done in their
lives. They long to spend time with God. They see
God at work, and while many are shown grace,
many do not appreciate it... blind to the splendor
of God. You hold your hand up high, but they
don't see it – open their eyes to what you do. Put
them to shame and light a fire beneath them...
get their attention. God grant us peace because
everything we have done, you have done for
us. Others have ruled us. You give life to the
living and death to the dead, the more life you
give the more glory you display. In trouble they
begged for help, but the discipline was so heavy
our prayers were whispers and labor birthed no

baby. In Jesus the dead will live, wake up and sing. The Earth will burst with life giving birth to the dead. Come my people, shut yourselves in for a while because God is sure to come and punish the wrong of this earth. Earth itself will point out the bloodstains, it will show where the murdered have been hidden away.

We Don't Quit

There are so many assignments God has given me that seemingly made no sense at the time. From moving from a dream job and dream home in Atlanta to an extended stay hotel in Virginia to planning a national conference in Atlanta when I had virtually no way to pay for it: God has asked me to do some incredible things. Nonetheless, all those things came to pass and blessed me in the end. He made the path level even though the vision was unclear. I imagine it was like leading a flock of people to the red sea with a hope that some how they would all make it across to safety. We must look to the sure signs of God when times get scary and uncertain. We must believe that God will make a way out of no way and will get the job done. Every assignment God has called me to, he has sent the provision and the power of the Holy Spirit to get me through.

"BLESSED BE THE LORD, THE GOD OF ISRAEL, FROM EVERLASTING EVEN TO EVERLASTING THEN ALL THE PEOPLE SAID, "AMEN," AND PRAISED THE LORD." I CHRONICLES 16:36

In Context

The Ark of the Covenant was in the center of David's tent. They began to worship God with burnt and peace offerings. He assigned some of the Levites to lead worship. They sang, "Thank God and call out his name! Tell the World who he is and what he has done! Sing to him and play songs for him. Revel in his Holy Name. Study God and his strength, seek his presence day and night. Remember his miracles, he keeps his commitments. He is God, our God – where you go come his judgments and decisions. He formed an eternal commitment to us. Even though we have journeyed from one land to the next, he didn't allow anyone to push us around. Praise God! Share the Gospel! Publish his glory among godless nations, his wonders to all races and religions.

Final Notes
Eternal blessings are ours to have and hold. We can give God all the praise right now. He will never lead us down a dark and dreary path. He is always defending and fighting for us. God will never let us down. In the light of day we give God glory honor and praise. We stand tall and believe in him. We trust him and we honor him. We desire what God desires and in this we know our work will not fail. We believe and trust him. Not only for today, but for eternity. We will live eternally with a God whose love, commitment and defense will never fail us. All we have to do is keep it pushing – trusting God.

A PRAYER TO MOVE YOUR MOUNTAIN

Most Gracious and Heavenly Father,

Lord we thank you for eternal gifts that never expire, never change, and never fail. You are our rock, our shield and our exceeding great reward. We can live a life for you, trusting that you are making a way out of no way to have your will accomplished. Lord be a fence all around us and help us to be all that you have created us to be. Lord, we thank you for choosing us and for saving us from a life of sin. Lord, we honor you, we love you, we seek you, we trust you and we praise you. Show us the path and we will walk. We will not give up. We will trust you.

In Jesus Name, Amen.

ABUNDANCE

Faith & Wisdom

MOVING YOUR MOUNTAIN

by stephanie d. moore

Nothing is bigger than our God! My sincere prayer is that this devotional has blessed you as much as it has blessed me, writing it. I have no idea what God has in store for us, but I am sure we have been ordained to become outstanding leaders for God. I pray that we each recognize and understand that the power of obedience will open doors no man can shut, keep us grounded in faith, allow us to shine in dark places and be a perfect conduit of God's message, love, mercy and grace. I love you and I am praying for your strength, perseverance, abundance and love.

May God Bless You and Keep You,

Stephanie Moore

www.ingramcontent.com/pod-product-compliance
Lightning Source LLC
Chambersburg PA
CBHW061721020426
42331CB00006B/1025